Yearni

For God

A Daily Devotional and Small Group Discipleship Resource

Volume 1

John D. Herman

Published by Rambling Star Publishing
Mechanicsville, VA
USA

ISBN-13: 978-0692023617 (Rambling Star Publishing)
ISBN-10: 0692023615

Cover Design by Heather Heckel

Cover Art Copyright Artur Bogacki | Dreamstime.com

Series Logo Art Copyright Twindesigner | Dreamstime.com

Also by John D. Herman

Going Deeper: A Journey with Jesus

God Comes to Us

Called to Follow

The Fruit of the Spirit

The Body of Christ

Acknowledgments

I give thanks… for your partnership in the gospel. This study guide has developed over several years of walking the faith together with the people of Peace Lutheran Church in Charlottesville, Virginia. We thank God for the deeper journey into which God has led us. I am especially grateful to the members of the Discipleship Team (Jenny Cudahy, Tom Czelusta, Deb Meyers, Dave Poole, Ruth Poole, and Nancy Schmitz) who have worked together with deep devotion to fulfill the dream of creating our own discipleship curriculum. Thanks also to Jennie Carter, Jean Dobbs, Kristin Langholz, and the several pilot groups who have provided helpful feedback for the revision of this first book of the series. My thanks also to the devotional writers, whose names appear in this volume, and who have graciously permitted the use of their reflections. I'm very grateful to Heather Heckel, whose decision to publish this series in a variety of formats will make it easily available to others on the journey. Finally, I thank my wife Leslie, who has lovingly and patiently supported me, and who is walking with me into a new life direction. *The peace of Christ be with you always* – John Herman.

Prologue

Going Deeper: A Journey with Jesus

How this Series Came to Be

Over the years, at conferences and workshops where we leaders of Peace Lutheran Church have led presentations about congregational spiritual growth and discipleship groups, we have been asked why we don't create our own discipleship curriculum. The answer is simple. The task has seemed overwhelming if not impossible. Where would we start? How would we do it? How could we come up with the people-hours necessary to write and produce such a resource? Besides, although not all of our participants were enthusiastically supportive of Greg Ogden's *Discipleship Essentials*, it still was the best discipleship workbook we could find (and could we actually improve upon that?).

Somewhere along the way (in other words, through the guidance of the Holy Spirit) we came up with an approach, and then a plan. What if we designed five worship and adult education series for 2011, so that they would provide the foundational material for our own discipleship curriculum? And that is what we did. We planned worship and education series (*Yearning for God; Who is This God We Believe In?; Come to the Water; Life on the Vine; The Body of Christ*), and asked congregational members to write daily devotions to accompany each series. Much of the material in this series is based on sermons, course content, and devotions from these worship series in 2011. As you read the chapters, you will notice names of people (members of Peace Lutheran Church, Charlottesville, VA) who wrote particular devotions to accompany the original worship series. When no name appears, the section was written by the author, John Herman.

How to Use this Resource

This discipleship series is intended for use by small groups and individuals, for people new to the faith as well as those who have grown up in the church. Although written by a Lutheran pastor for a Lutheran congregation, the resource invites a wider mainline Christian audience. The series is designed to promote daily quiet time dedicated to being in the Word, study, and prayer, spiritual disciplines that promote the work of the Holy Spirit in your life. There are typically six days of readings in each chapter. You will get more out of it when you read and reflect daily rather than trying to cover an entire week in one or two sessions.

You will also get more out of it by using this resource together in a small group of 3-6 people. I am convinced that faith grows best in the context of small groups. That is, we are more likely to be growing spiritually when walking together with other disciples. Making disciples involves developing significant Christ-centered relationships, and that happen in small groups.

Small groups will want to use the final chapter section: *Taking It Further: Small Group and Chapter Summary Questions*, as a starting point for their weekly discussions. Begin together with a review of Chapter Eleven (Small Group Guidelines), and decide about a small group covenant. Further suggestions and strategy for using this series can be found in *Chapter Ten: Next Steps*. The subsequent books of the series can be found at your favorite online bookstore in ebook and print formats.

Why I Believe in Small Groups

After thirty years of pastoral ministry, I've come to the conclusion that a small group ministry is essential for churches that want to grow disciples. They are not just an add-on for those people who might be interested in them. Following the pattern of the early church in Acts 2:42-47, small groups should be an essential structure of the church.

It is my hope that you will use this resource with a small group of 2-5 other people. Consider these essential benefits brought about by small groups. Small groups using this resource will:

help grow Christians deeper in Jesus Christ;

encourage the daily spiritual disciplines of Bible reading, prayer, and meditation;

connect people to each other and build close relationships;

And not only that, but small groups can also help to foster a culture of discipleship within congregations. Small groups:

help a congregation move toward more authentic relationships. Churches usually remain on the level of casual acquaintance without them.

help to foster honesty and transparency in congregational relationships;

broaden the care ministry of the congregation;

change people…and changed people change congregations.

Introduction to *Yearning for God*

The first book of the series, *Going Deeper: A Journey with Jesus*, begins with the human yearning of the creature to know the Creator (chapters one and two). The study guide then progresses through several life-changing encounters of people with Jesus Christ (Nicodemus, the Samaritan woman at the well, the blind man, the woman caught in adultery, the woman who washed Jesus' feet with her tears, Peter, and a few would-be followers). As we study their interactions with Jesus, we see Jesus speak to their hearts and touch their lives, and these people are never the same.

I hope that this book will be a helpful companion for a wide variety of people, for people new to the Christian faith as well as those who have grown up in the church. May you be led to know the Living Water that quenches your deep thirst, and in knowing him, may your life never be the same.

What is Discipleship?

If we are going to spend ten weeks or a year or more studying discipleship, we had better begin with a definition. Discipleship is learning to follow Jesus. Learning to live the way of Jesus. Learning to live by the Spirit. For those who desire a more technical definition, discipleship to Jesus Christ is "the intentional, communal, lifelong journey of being conformed to Jesus Christ through the power of the Holy Spirit to accomplish God's purpose in the world."[1]

Chapter One: Yearning for Meaning

Please note: If you are using this discipleship resource in a small group, please have the small group review* ***Chapter Eleven: Small Group Guidelines* *together at the beginning of your time together.*

Brian McLaren, well-known contemporary Christian author, before he was a pastor, was a college English teacher. He tells the story about how one day he arrived at the small school to find the lights off, and no one around. He walked down to the office, where he found one of his colleagues sitting there, who, laughing, motioned McLaren to sit down, and said,

"So you and I are the only idiots who didn't know that classes were canceled today."

They realized that classes must have been canceled due to the building renovations, and as McLaren got up to leave, his colleague asked,

"Hey Brian, can I ask you a personal question?"

His colleague, Bill, had a PhD in Philosophy, and he had been ribbing McLaren since he found out that McLaren was a committed Christian. So McLaren was not surprised when Bill asked,

"What's a nice guy like you doing in a disgusting religion like Christianity?"

McLaren laughed and responded, "What kind of question is that to hit me with at 8:00 AM on a Monday morning?" Then his cynical colleague seemed to get tears in his eyes.

"Brian, can we talk for a minute?" McLaren nodded.

"You know me. You know I have a real problem with this God thing. Well – and you're the first person I've told this to – two weeks ago I admitted that I have an alcohol problem, and I've been sober for two weeks – the longest period of sobriety I've had since I was about 13. When I got here about a half hour ago, I was terrified. I thought – oh no, I have a whole day on my hands with nothing to do – and I felt the urge to go out and drink. AA keeps telling me about this Higher Power bit, but I don't buy it yet. But then I prayed anyway, and right after that, you walk in the door. Kind of spooky, huh?"

They went out to breakfast together, where they shared their life stories, and they hung out together until the day's first AA meeting, which they also attended together.[2]

We begin with the place where most every discussion about religion begins, with the relationship between God and human beings. Are human beings naturally religious? Is there something about the essence of humanity that longs to know that which is transcendent (that which is other-worldly and beyond ordinary human experience)? At the very least, it seems we humans need to believe there is meaning to life. "Social scientists tell us that the greatest threat to humanity is the discovery that life is meaningless…We can withstand almost any tragedy – devastation, loss, heartache, oppression – so long as we can make sense of it."[3]

Perhaps that is one consequence in the Genesis creation story (Genesis 1:26-31) where humanity is created in the *image of God.* Craig Barnes claims that the indelible mark of the image of God upon humanity serves two functions. "The first is that it is the source of our hunger for life's meaning, and the second is that it refuses to be satisfied with any meaning other than the eternal."[4] Is it because we are created in God's image that we creatures long to be connected to the Creator?

In his book, *Mere Christianity*, C. S. Lewis offers this analogy. "If the whole universe has no meaning, we should never have found out that it has no meaning – just as, if there were no light in the universe and therefore no creatures with eyes, we should never know it was dark. Dark would be without meaning. Similarly, the fact that eyes exist suggests that light must exist. And the fact that we have spiritual longings…the fact that we even have a meaningful category of thought and speech called spirituality…suggests that there is some corresponding reality out there which we have the capacity to 'sense.' That capacity would be called faith, and that reality, God."[5]

C. S. Lewis is saying that if human beings have "a seemingly incurable, innate, core hunger and thirst for spiritual meaning," then that is at least evidence that there may be a reality corresponding to the desire.[6]

Day 1: The Unknown God

> ***Acts 17:16-33*** *While Paul was waiting for them in Athens, he was deeply distressed to see that the city was full of idols. [17]So he argued in the synagogue with the Jews and the devout persons, and also in the marketplace every day with those who happened to be there. [18]Also some Epicurean and Stoic philosophers debated with him. Some said, "What does this babbler want to say?" Others said, "He seems to be a proclaimer of foreign divinities." (This was because he was telling the good news about Jesus and the resurrection.) [19]So they took him and brought him to the Areopagus and asked him, "May we know what this new teaching is that you are presenting? [20]It sounds rather strange to us, so we would like to know what it means." [21]Now all the Athenians and the foreigners living there would spend their time in nothing but telling or hearing something new. [22]Then Paul stood in front of the Areopagus and said, "Athenians, I see how extremely religious you are in every way. [23]For as I went through the city and looked carefully at the objects of your worship, I found among them an altar with the inscription, 'To an unknown god.' What therefore you worship as unknown, this I proclaim to you. [24]The God who made the world and everything in it, he who is Lord of heaven and earth, does not live in shrines made by human hands, [25]nor is he served by human hands, as though he needed anything, since he himself gives to all mortals life and breath and all things. [26]From one ancestor he made all nations to inhabit the whole earth, and he allotted the times of their existence and the boundaries of the places where they would live, [27]so that they would search for God and perhaps grope for him and find him – though indeed he is not far from each one of us. [28]For 'In him we live and move and have our being'; as even some of your own poets have said, 'For we too are his offspring.' [29]Since we are God's offspring, we ought not to think that the deity is like gold, or silver, or stone, an image formed by the art and imagination of*

mortals. 30While God has overlooked the times of human ignorance, now he commands all people everywhere to repent, 31because he has fixed a day on which he will have the world judged in righteousness by a man whom he has appointed, and of this he has given assurance to all by raising him from the dead." 32When they heard of the resurrection of the dead, some scoffed; but others said, "We will hear you again about this." 33At that point Paul left them.

The city of Athens, in the Apostle Paul's day, was a city of idols. The presence of so many idols seems to reveal that the people had a deep spiritual hunger. After some Athenians heard Paul's preaching, he was asked to present his teaching at the Areopagus. (The Athenians loved to discuss the latest new ideas.)

Paul begins by acknowledging their spirituality. They are religious people. Paul compliments their interest in spiritual things. At least they are searching. They know that something more is needed to bring meaning to life. Among their objects of worship and devotion Paul finds an altar with the inscription, "To An Unknown God."[7] Paul refers to this altar to an unknown god to introduce the God of all. (This unknown god is the one I've come to tell you about. I have come to declare to you the God whom you have unknowingly and ignorantly worshiped for years.)[8]

Today and tomorrow, we will focus on what Paul tells the Athenians about God. The first thing Paul proclaims about God (Acts 17:24-25) is that there is one God who is the maker of the world and everything in it. This God is not created by human hands. This God created humans and all that exists. Whereas paganism taught that the gods demand gifts from human beings, this God does not need anything from people; rather, this God gives people their life and breath and all good gifts. This God does not live in shrines made by human hands. This God does not need to live in a temple. This God created the universe and everything in it, and can be known to some extent through the creation around us.

Questions for reflection:

What alternate gods or idols do people in our world worship? (Let's suppose that an idol or god is something that draws our minds and hearts away from God.)

How might pondering the order and mysteries of our world move one toward faith in God?

to begin the conversation is to participate, even passively

→ to enter the theatre to hear the musician – or pause to hear the street musician and give attention is to give opportunity.

Faith is much the same.

Prayer: *As I begin this discipleship study, I pray that it will be a season of opening to you, O Lord, that I may receive what you have for me, and grow in areas that you intend. All for your purpose, in Jesus Christ, Amen.*

Day 2: Drawn to the One Who Made Us

> ***Acts 17:26-27*** *"From one ancestor he made all nations to inhabit the whole earth,*
> *and he allotted the times of their existence and the boundaries of the places where*
> *they would live,* 27 *so that they would search for God and perhaps grope for him and*
> *find him – though indeed he is not far from each one of us."*

The second thing that Paul tells the Athenians about God is that God wants to draw all of humanity to himself. The Athenians were used to gods who dwelt on Mount Olympus, and who were remote from humanity. "People had to go through perilous journeys to find the gods and placate them. But the true and living God has reached out to humanity."[9] This God is Lord of all history. This God created all nations from one ancestor and guided their histories, and arranged their events so that human beings might find him, ("so that they would search for God and perhaps grope for him and find him-- though indeed he is not far from each one of us"). Paul is saying that we are made in the image of this God and this God comes to us, and we have a capacity to respond to this God. We are made for God, and it is God's intention that human beings seek him.

The third thing Paul tells the Athenians about God is that God not only reveals himself in his works, but also in his word. The word, for example, that Paul is preaching to them. God has overlooked human ignorance, but now that they have heard the truth, it is time to repent (which means to turn to God; 17:30-31). Paul is cautioning the Athenians that they risk missing the relationship and life God intends for them. Consider it this way. What are they risking if they surrender their lives in trust to God? (They risk being wrong…that God is not the Creator and God of all.) But what are they risking if they don't turn to God? (They risk missing the life God intends for them, and all that goes with it. They risk separation from God their Creator.)

Finally, Paul speaks very briefly about Jesus Christ, mentioning his resurrection from death, an event that is completely contrary to their knowledge of the world and the way the world works. Paul is claiming that this God is Lord even over death. To this word about resurrection, some Athenians mocked Paul's words; some were willing to hear more about it; and others responded in faith to Paul's message, and put their trust in the God of all. They came to realize that this God is the one they have been seeking all along.

Questions for reflection:

Have you experienced being drawn to your Creator God? If so, how did this happen?

As I look back over my life, particularly in family, church, youth group, friends, biblical study & opportunity, camps, etc. I see God repeatedly pulling me, persuing me, calling me and drawing close that I might seen him and beleive.

Has God revealed himself to you in particular ways? How so?

Yes, in Words of people, circumstances, Bible, sacraments

profoundly so

Why do you think that the resurrection of Jesus Christ can be a stumbling block for people?

It challenges what we see as normal, our expectations and thus understanding/belief about reality

We rely on our understanding of reality to make decisions and self-perceive – losing this means we lose control over our reality.

thus faith in someone outside ourselves.

Prayer: *Draw me to yourself, O Lord, in a way that I may know what it is to be truly at home. Amen.*

Gracious God, grant that I might know you and your closeness. Grant me faith to know. Never let me go nor relent drawing me to yourself. This I ask by Christ's grace.

Amen.

Day 3: Real Nourishment

> ***Isaiah 55:1-2, 6-12.*** *Ho, everyone who thirsts, come to the waters; and you that have*
> *no money, come, buy and eat! Come, buy wine and milk without money and without*
> *price. Why do you spend your money for that which is not bread, and your labor for*
> *that which does not satisfy? Listen carefully to me, and eat what is good, and delight*
> *yourselves in rich food....6Seek the LORD while he may be found, call upon him*
> *while he is near; 7let the wicked forsake their way, and the unrighteous their*
> *thoughts; let them return to the LORD, that he may have mercy on them, and to our*
> *God, for he will abundantly pardon. 8For my thoughts are not your thoughts, nor are*
> *your ways my ways, says the LORD. 9For as the heavens are higher than the earth,*
> *so are my ways higher than your ways and my thoughts than your thoughts. 10For as*
> *the rain and the snow come down from heaven, and do not return there until they*
> *have watered the earth, making it bring forth and sprout, giving seed to the sower*
> *and bread to the eater, 11so shall my word be that goes out from my mouth; it shall*
> *not return to me empty, but it shall accomplish that which I purpose, and succeed in*
> *the thing for which I sent it. 12For you shall go out in joy, and be led back in peace;*
> *the mountains and the hills before you shall burst into song, and all the trees of the*
> *field shall clap their hands.*

The prophet Isaiah cautions against spending money on that which is not bread, and working for that which does not satisfy, as if we are trying to subsist on junk food and missing the real nourishment. Jesus says much the same thing in John 6:27: "Do not work for the food that perishes, but for the food that endures for eternal life." How do we work and live for the food that perishes? We attempt to fill our lives with the meaning and fulfillment we sense is missing. "This craving to fill life's empty places forms the cosmic axis around which our world turns. No matter where the search leads us – through one relationship after another, through job after job, into therapy, recreation, and achievements, and even through different churches – we continue to believe this next thing will fulfill us."[10]

Questions for reflection:

What things have you given your money to or even your life that have ultimately proven to be unfulfilling? Distracting? Disappointing?

What does it mean to *seek the Lord?*

I wish I knew more fully.

Surely to read his Word; to practice of faith in action; to live in His world view and perspective...

But to seek... I only know he is in the sacraments and so to them I cling.

I know He speaks through his Word and so I read.

Perhaps I know what it is to seek, but often struggle to find.

What does it mean to live according to the Word of God? (Matthew 4:4 and Deuteronomy 8:3)

We do live according to God's grace and provision, even if we do not perceive it. And that provision is his word for us.

I wish I would hear and perceive more the word and heart behind beyond the grace.

To know the heart & will & mind of the God in, through, behind Christ the Word.

written word < spoken word < living word

Prayer: *Gracious God, your blessed Son came down from heaven to be the true bread that gives life to the world. Give us this bread always, that he may live in us and we in him, and that, strengthened by this food, we may live as his body in the world, through Jesus Christ, our Savior and Lord. Amen.*[11]

Day 4: Is This All There Is?

Is this all there is? That was the inner question I often felt as a child on Christmas Day after all the presents had been unwrapped, the toys and presents had been taken to my bedroom, and the wrapping paper and bows had been thrown into the garbage. I never spoke the question aloud, but it was always there, every Christmas, every year. Is this all there is? Don't misunderstand. I wasn't wishing that I had more presents to open. I always received many more gifts than any child could have desired or expected. What I was feeling had more to do with a sense of inner emptiness. A deep realization that the gifts didn't do it. As nice as they were, they just didn't carry the weight. They didn't make Christmas into the special (read "spiritual") event that it was supposed to be.

As I moved into adulthood, I began to see that we try to load a lot of baggage and expectations unto Christmas, trying to make it into something that it can never be. And I also began to see that the inner feeling that something was missing (is this all there is?) was one of the first clues that I did not have the ability to give my life the meaning it craved. I came to understand this statement of Craig Barnes: "Our gospel scandalously claims that we are never going to get life together for ourselves, and the harder we try the further we will roam from the God of grace. At the heart of Christianity is the confession that we are completely at the mercy of God to receive life and meaning."[12]

Questions for Reflection:

What does Craig Barnes mean that we will "never get our life together for ourselves?"

When left to our own efforts, devices, intentions, etc. the outcome is plain to see on TV news. The power of sin and brokeness is too strong and pervasive within.

What does he mean that we are completely "at the mercy of God to receive both life and life's meaning?"

Just that; the words bring perspective to the desperation of our life.

Ecclesiastes 1:12-18. *I, the Teacher, when king over Israel in Jerusalem,* [13] *applied my mind to seek and to search out by wisdom all that is done under heaven; it is an unhappy business that God has given to human beings to be busy with.* [14] *I saw all the deeds that are done under the sun; and see, all is vanity and a chasing after wind.* [15] *What is crooked cannot be made straight, and what is lacking cannot be counted.* [16] *I said to myself, "I have acquired great wisdom, surpassing all who were over Jerusalem before me; and my mind has had great experience of wisdom and knowledge."* [17] *And I applied my mind to know wisdom and to know madness and folly. I perceived that this also is but a chasing after wind.* [18] *For in much wisdom is much vexation, and those who increase knowledge increase sorrow.*

What are some of this author's conclusions about life? How do you agree or disagree with these conclusions?

We will in our broken carnal nature be attacked by lusts and temptations, lies of dissatisfaction, ill-contentment all which will leave us empty in the end. They are real and yet result in chasing after the wind.

Ultimately, we are desperate for God's mercy and fulfilment.

Day 5: Yearning for Faith (Nancy Schmitz)

> ***Hebrews 11:1-3*** *Now faith is the assurance of things hoped for, the conviction of things not seen. [2]Indeed, by faith our ancestors received approval. [3]By faith we understand that the worlds were prepared by the word of God, so that what is seen was made from things that are not visible.*

Do you ever have those times when you feel like you are holding on by a thin strand for dear life and wish there was just one thing for sure that you could depend on? There are two things for certain in life. First, life is unpredictable. No matter how hard you try you can't control everything. Your computer may crash, your car battery may die, your family may feud, your job may be downsized, your friend may move away, your spouse may be unfaithful, or an injury or illness may sideline you or a loved one. And none of it may be your fault. But there is one thing you can count on – God will always be there for you, good times or bad, and he will never forsake you. That you can count on! The prophet Zephaniah assures us "The Lord your God is with you, he is mighty to save. He will take great delight in you, he will quiet you with his love, he will rejoice over you with singing" (Zephaniah 3:17).

Faith is the foundation of our relationship with God. Hebrews 11:1 says that "faith is being sure of what we hope for and certain of what we do not see." It is knowing that God created you, provides for you, and empowers you. It is not just a belief in your head, but a knowing in your heart. It means that you learn to trust in God no matter what your circumstances. Sometimes it takes something bad to happen before we are willing to turn to God to guide and sustain us. Brokenness is often the entry point for faith to take a foothold. But it needs nurturing to grow. It deepens as we spend more time with God in his word, sacrament, and prayer. It develops the more we wrestle together with other faithful people through our doubts, questions, and difficult times. It blossoms and bears fruit the more we allow it to permeate all aspects of our life.

Questions for reflection:

What events in the unpredictability of your life have been most difficult to face?

There most certainly have been unwanted and unexpected events in life. Moments of sheer desperation as a mortal throws themself upon the mercy of God. Yet is not this also ongoing. It too often feels like the desperation due to some measure of brokenness is normal.

Of all the moments, my time as a canoe guy taught me the most about dependence and mercy, and perhaps faith. Thank you for bringing me through those moments.

At what times in your life have you felt most strongly that God is with you? (Offer a prayer of thanks for these times.)

When His Word speaks.

Thank you for your Word- it is water to my dry soul.

How does doubt affect your faith?

It attacks constantly. It als bolsters and teaches.

It pushes to new levels of faith as God gives once again.

What do you think about Nancy's statement: "Brokenness is often the entry point for faith to take a foothold?" How has that truth played out in your life?

Brokenness and Law drive us to Christ.

My brokeness leads me to depend on, seek out, and learn more from Christ...

Day 6: Great Is Your Faithfulness (Nancy Schmitz)

It was not a pretty time in my life. A co-worker had resigned which meant longer hours for me, my husband was working out of town, I had two preschoolers and was pregnant again, and my babysitter told me she couldn't keep the kids anymore. I felt like I was stressed to my limit or beyond. I thought I could sustain nothing more. Then in a matter of two months two catastrophes happened that turned me from feeling like I was drowning to knowing I was on sure ground and not forsaken. First, our house was hit by lightning. An intense storm came off the mountains with especially severe lightning. My husband and I looked at each other with an uneasy feeling and he decided he'd better go upstairs and unplug his computer. Not five minutes later there was an intense boom that shook the house, the electricity went out and we knew we had been hit. We gathered the kids, called the fire department and got out of the house. The lightning blew a corner out of the upstairs room where the computer was. Amazingly there was no fire, no one was hurt, and help quickly fell into place to get things fixed.

Just two months later during an early snowstorm, I was driving along and saw a red light ahead. I prepared to stop but my brakes locked, throwing me into a skid, so that I crashed head on into a telephone pole. I was taken by ambulance to the Emergency Room. I was 5 months pregnant at the time but amazingly neither I nor the baby was seriously hurt.

That year, I felt like the Israelites wandering in the desert. I didn't know how I was going to make it. Then the lightning hit, the car smashed, and it pulled me right up and I immediately knew how I was going to make it – not by my strength but by God's provision. I thanked God that the lightning didn't strike five minutes earlier when my husband was in the room. I thanked God for supplying a good contractor to get the repairs to the house done quickly. I thanked God that I was alive and walking and talking and still had a healthy baby. It could have been so much worse. I thanked God for his blessings.

It was faith that sustained me at that time and allowed me to respond with thanksgiving in the midst of disaster. And it is faith that continues to sustain me today.

> *"The Lord is my rock, my fortress and my deliverer;*
> *my God is my rock, in whom I take refuge,*
> *my shield and the horn of my salvation.*
> *He is my stronghold, my refuge and my savior." (2 Samuel 22:1-3)*

Questions for reflection:

Sometimes we think that following Jesus ought to protect us from experiencing crisis and pain. But our lives show us a different reality. What impact did difficult events have on your faith?

I echo the words above – moments of crisis in my life have also been moments of provision, protection, radical growth, etc.

I am not sure if my faith is "stronger" but ~~I am certainly~~ it is demanded of me through these events to trust more.

I love this.

✱ Someone once said, ✱"It's not the greatness of my faith, but it's my faith in the greatness of God.✱" What important distinction was this person making?

faith reveals God's activity, God's grace, God's activity. My faith is poor and week but his greatness compensates exponentially.

Nancy likened her experience to the Israelites wandering in the wilderness. Read Deuteronomy 8:1-20. What are some of the things the Israelites should have learned on their wilderness journey?

the Lord is the one who gives "the power to be successful" – He is the actor, giver.

Therefore be humble; know yourself and you finitude that you might know God's infitnate nature.

Closing Prayer: *God of all, I acknowledge that underneath most of my desires I have desired you, and that the meaning I have sought is found in you. So draw me to yourself that I may be truly at home. Amen.*

I confess in desiring you I have sought other god's, other fulfillment. Forgive me.

By your grace of your Son, think of me, and contince your work through and in me

May we follow your love, law, commands and will Lord.

Amen.

Taking It Further: Small Group and Chapter Summary Questions

(The questions at the end of each chapter have two purposes. If you are using this resource individually, these questions will help to summarize the week's study. If you are using this resource as a small group, these questions are a good starting point for group discussion. See **Preface: Small Group Guidelines** for guidance about using these questions. If the small group has not yet developed a covenant, this first meeting would be a good time to do so.)

What do you think…do humans naturally believe there is (or should be) meaning to life?

Everyone, at some point in their life, at least wonders

Do you think doubt is the opposite of faith or the friend of faith?

I do not know - but I beleive God's call and activity is greater than our doubt.

In Psalm 42:11, the psalmist speaks about a disquiet in his soul. What is that like?

You know

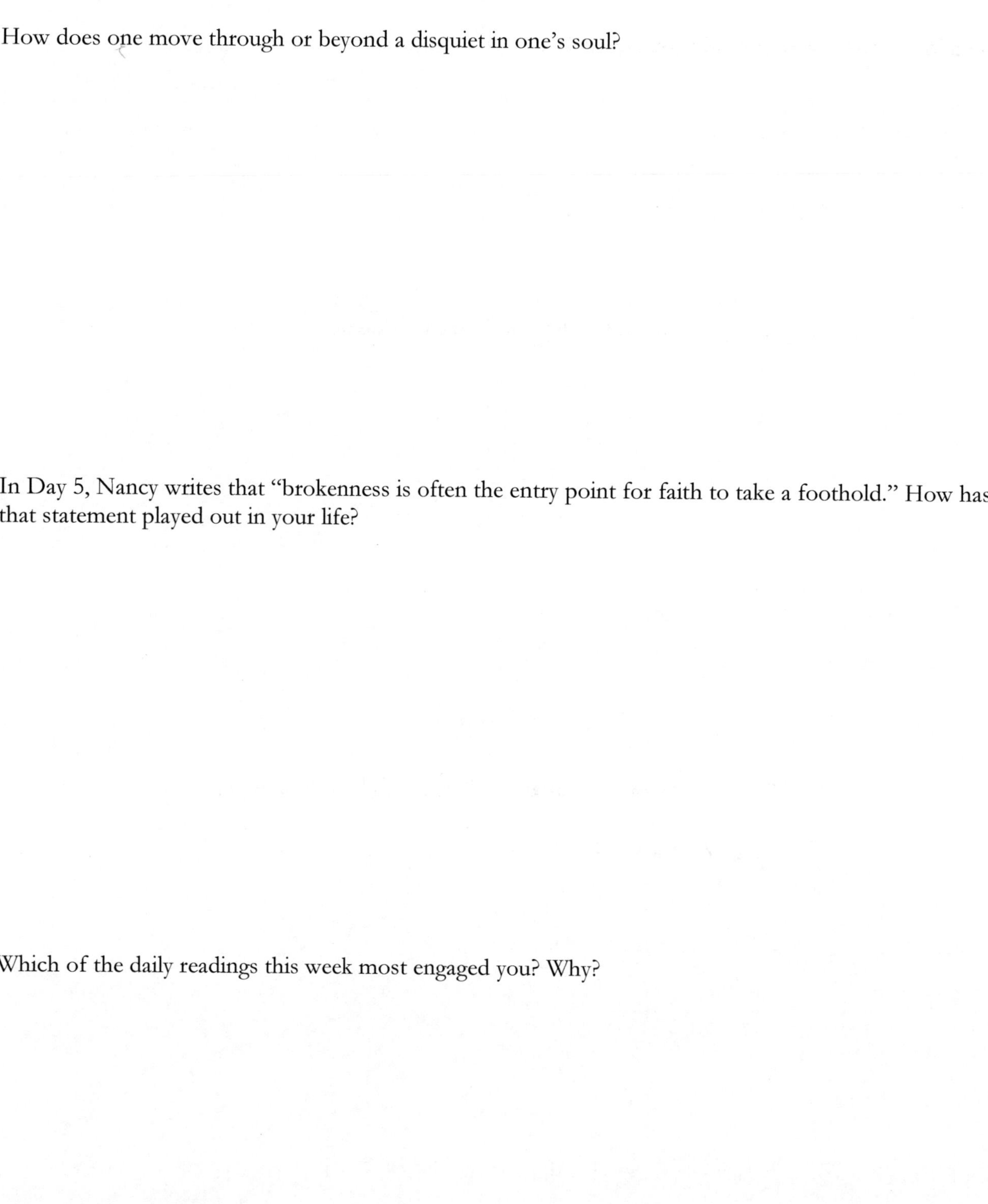

How does one move through or beyond a disquiet in one's soul?

In Day 5, Nancy writes that "brokenness is often the entry point for faith to take a foothold." How has that statement played out in your life?

Which of the daily readings this week most engaged you? Why?

What questions or issues would you like to discuss with others?

Which of the Bible readings took on a new meaning for you this week?

What do you want to remember from this chapter?

A biblical reading to remember: **Isaiah 55:2** *Why do you spend your money for that which is not bread, and your labor for that which does not satisfy? Listen carefully to me, and eat what is good, and delight yourselves in rich food.*

Recommended resources for further study:

M. Craig Barnes, *Yearning: Living Between How It is & How It Ought To Be*

Brian McLaren, *Finding Faith: A Search for What Is Real*

Brian McLaren, *Finding Faith: A Search for What Makes Sense*

Henri Nouwen, *A Cry For Mercy: Prayers from the Genesee*

Lucinda Vardey, *Mother Teresa: A Simple Path*

Chapter Two: Yearning for Relationship

Human beings not only have a deep longing for meaning, but also have a related longing for connection. We are created for relationship: relationship to God, to each other, and to the world around us. We find our meaning in being loved and loving others. We yearn for love, for unconditional love. There is in us a deep yearning to know God and to know that God loves us.

Day 1: Restless Hearts

Several times in the Psalms, the author likens his longing for God to a deep thirst:

> ***Psalm 42:1*** *"As a deer longs for flowing streams, so my soul longs for you, O God."*
>
> ***Psalm 63:1*** *"O God, you are my God, I seek you, my soul thirsts for you; my flesh faints for you, as in a dry and weary land where there is no water."*

In Psalm 42, the longing for God is compared to a deer roaming the desert land of Palestine in search of a drink of water from a spring or wadi.

What does it mean that one's soul thirsts for God?

The prayers of the psalmist lead us to remember two later oft quoted statements which describe the longing of the human soul that feels the emptiness of life apart from God. Augustine (354-430) said, "Thou hast made us for Thyself, O Lord, and our hearts are restless until they rest in Thee." And many centuries later, Blaise Pascal (1623-1662) said, "There is a God shaped vacuum in the heart of every man which cannot be filled by any created thing, but only by God, the Creator, made known through Jesus."

The words of Psalm 42 suggest that the psalmist is away from the temple in Jerusalem, but would love to be present in the Lord's house with the other worshipers. The psalmist remembers fondly how he joined the procession of worshipers to the temple, and even led the way. What an inspiring time it was, shouting and singing songs of thanksgiving to God! So why am I now depressed, wonders the psalmist? I trust the day will come when I shall make the pilgrimage once again to join with the other worshipers in the presence of God. But for now my soul is cast down. I feel far from God. Yet I will praise You because you are my only hope, even here where I am far away from the temple. Notice how the psalmist moves through the dry times (when he feels distant from God), to a trust that he would once again enjoy the presence of God. "Hope in God; for I shall again praise him, my help and my God." (Psalm 42:5-6)

Questions for reflection:

Take a look inside. What is the deep thirst, what is the deep longing of your soul?

Having "tasted and seen" I long for that divine intimacy with Christ – with our Triune God.

Have you gone through times when you longed for God's presence in a deep way? Times when your soul has been cast down and disquieted? What were they?

Yes - both in times of great sorrow and trial, as well in times of monotany and grinding status quo.

What were the outcomes?

I learn patience and trust. He provides what I need in the moment, but there is still the longing.

It is almost like I am being taught how to be content with the ever present ever pressing desire for his increased closeness - where it is normal to be suspended apart yet pursuing one another.

Prayer: "*As a deer longs for flowing streams, so my soul longs for you, O God.*" (Psalm 42:1)

Day 2: Yearning for Love (Deb Meyers)

Proverbs 19:22 *"What a person desires is unfailing love."*

We yearn for love. We yearn to be connected, to be valued, to be accepted for who we are, to be loved unconditionally. We yearn for a love that doesn't fail or disappoint us. That kind of love seems so elusive, so hard to find.

The world tells us we are not good enough, not pretty or handsome enough, not smart enough, not rich enough, not successful enough. We are bombarded by messages telling us what to buy and what to do to make ourselves more loveable, more desirable. We often buy into this notion and go searching after that "more," only to end up feeling more empty and unloved than before.

And if this is not enough, we even tell ourselves that we are undesirable, unworthy, unforgivable, too messed up to be loved like we yearn to be loved. We may be able to fool the world, but inside, we know exactly how unlovable we are and why. We replay our past mistakes and believe our own messages of self-condemnation.

God tells us something different. God points to a different reality. God tells us that we are loved with His unfailing love; that we are accepted, chosen, forgiven, and redeemed. He is our rock--the one we can cling to, the one we can count on, the one who loves us and says he will never let us go. In demonstration of that love, God sent Jesus to be the Savior of the world.

Questions for reflection:

Who does the world say you are?

the world says I am a misguided but well-intentioned do gooder who never lives up to the fake ideals I perpetuate.

Who does God say you are? Can you think of scriptural verses which tell you who God says you are?

Child

I think of the scripture that says a "spirit of sonship," adoption.

As much as I am his child, though, I fear I make him wearisome, frustrated, tired, etc.

I don't like failing him or others - particularly should it reflect poorly upon him.

Romans 8:31-39. *What then are we to say about these things? If God is for us, who is against us?* [32]*He who did not*
withhold his own Son, but gave him up for all of us, will he not with him also give us everything else?... [35]*Who will*
separate us from the love of Christ? Will hardship, or distress, or persecution, or famine, or nakedness, or peril, or
sword?... [37]*No, in all these things we are more than conquerors through him who loved us.* [38]*For I am convinced that*
neither death, nor life, nor angels, nor rulers, nor things present, nor things to come, nor powers, [39]*nor height, nor depth,*
nor anything else in all creation, will be able to separate us from the love of God in Christ Jesus our Lord.

What promise about God's love is proclaimed by Paul? In what other scriptures have you heard the promise of God's unfailing love? Give thanks to God for those promises.

In the sacraments I find the promise of his unfailing unending love.

Day 3: We Yearn for Love, Even When It's Undeserved (Deb Meyers)

Have you ever felt ashamed or unworthy of love, because of things you've said or done in the past? Does self-condemnation or the condemnation of others keep you trapped in darkness and defeat? Do you wonder why God or anyone else might want to love you, given how often you've messed up? Read the following and be reminded of God's compassion and mercy; God's desire for us to repent (to return to him); and God's desire that we receive forgiveness and experience his unfailing love.

> ***Romans 5:8*** *But God proves his love for us in that while we still were sinners Christ died for us.*
>
> ***Isaiah 43:25*** *I am He who blots out your transgressions for my own sake, and I will not remember your sins.*
>
> ***Luke 15:7*** *Just so, I tell you, there will be more joy in heaven over one sinner who repents than over ninety-nine righteous persons who need no repentance.*

If you were to do a word search in the Bible (NIV translation), you would see that the term "unfailing love" appears 40 times. It's interesting that in every instance, the phrase refers to God's love for us, imperfect human beings. The love of others can be very powerful, but only God's love is unfailing.

I am deeply blessed (and I'm sure you are too) with many people (and pets) who love me dearly. But I find comfort in the fact that no matter what losses or hurts I may still experience in this life, I can always count on the unfailing love of God. God was with me when I breathed my first breath and he'll be with me when I breathe my last. God will never leave me, nor forsake me (Hebrews 13:5). In God, I have the gift of unfailing love. Allow this promise to be the source of your thoughts (your meditation) today.

Questions for reflection:

Who are the people in your life who have dearly loved you? Whom have you dearly loved?

I think of love so much as commitment and decision. But there is something more there too. In this I think of my love for my child - imperfect as I am.

As special as their love is for you, or your love for them, do you realize that God loves you with an even deeper love? What does it mean to you that God's love for you is both unconditional and unfailing?

It is something sometimes easy to see and know. I can logically point to it. But it also takes a great deal of faith to believe its there.

Prayer: *Thank you, Lord, for your unfailing, unconditional, undeserved, love for me. Amen.*

Day 4: God Is with Us

> ***Matthew 1:18-23*** *Now the birth of Jesus the Messiah took place in this way. When his mother Mary had been engaged to Joseph, but before they lived together, she was found to be with child from the Holy Spirit.* [19]*Her husband Joseph, being a righteous man and unwilling to expose her to public disgrace, planned to dismiss her quietly.* [20]*But just when he had resolved to do this, an angel of the Lord appeared to him in a dream and said, "Joseph, son of David, do not be afraid to take Mary as your wife, for the child conceived in her is from the Holy Spirit. She will bear a son, and you are to name him Jesus, for he will save his people from their sins." All this took place to fulfill what had been spoken by the Lord through the prophet: "Look, the virgin shall conceive and bear a son, and they shall name him Emmanuel," which means, "God is with us."*

The baby that is to be born to Mary and Joseph is given two names. He is to be named **Jesus** because he will save his people. The Hebrew name "Jesus" is the verb "to save." What will he save his people from? Later we learn Jesus will save people from sin and guilt, from death and destruction, and from despair and hopelessness. His name is Jesus, because he is the savior. Why do we need a savior? Because we cannot save ourselves.

His second name is to be **Emmanuel**, which means "God is with us." Where the name Emmanuel is used in Isaiah 7:14, the prophet reassures Jerusalem that she would not be abandoned to her enemies, because the Lord was with her to defend her. Now the same name is given to Jesus, for in Jesus is God's presence and power to save his people. In Jesus God is decisively present in the world to make everything new. The birth of the child Jesus is the announcement that we are not alone.[13]

At the beginning of Matthew's gospel, we learn something not only about Jesus, but also about ourselves. The announcement of the birth of Jesus reminds us that we need a savior (he will be called **Jesus**), and that we are dependent on God for our lives (and therefore Jesus is also **Emmanuel** – God is with us). Right away in Matthew's gospel we hear the message of God's grace, that in Jesus God comes to us, in our brokenness, to save us. Jesus is the one who saves. And in Jesus we come to know God, Emmanuel. From the beginning, God has been saying to the world: I love you. And in Jesus that word becomes flesh. In Jesus, Love becomes human.

Questions for reflection:

What does it mean to you that Jesus is both Savior and Emmanuel?

Interesting that these are names, not simply titles. This is who He is.

God with us, revealed, is not vengeful or hateful, but loving to the point of self-sacrifice – saving us from the very destruction we have wrought.

What other names for Jesus are important in your relationship to him? Allow these names of Jesus to develop into a prayer.

Master, friend, shepherd, teacher

Day 5: Conversion of the Heart

> ***John 21:15-19*** *When they had finished breakfast, Jesus said to Simon Peter, "Simon*
> *son of John, do you love me more than these?" He said to him, "Yes, Lord; you*
> *know that I love you." Jesus said to him, "Feed my lambs." 16A second time he said*
> *to him, "Simon son of John, do you love me?" He said to him, "Yes, Lord; you know*
> *that I love you." Jesus said to him, "Tend my sheep." 17He said to him the third time,*
> *"Simon son of John, do you love me?" Peter felt hurt because he said to him the*
> *third time, "Do you love me?" And he said to him, "Lord, you know everything; you*
> *know that I love you." Jesus said to him, "Feed my sheep. 18Very truly, I tell you,*
> *when you were younger, you used to fasten your own belt and to go wherever you*
> *wished. But when you grow old, you will stretch out your hands, and someone else*
> *will fasten a belt around you and take you where you do not wish to go." 19(He said*
> *this to indicate the kind of death by which he would glorify God.) After this he said to*
> *him, "Follow me."*

Many times I am frustrated with how small my commitment to live for Jesus is, and how far I have yet to travel in giving him my whole life. I need his constant forgiveness and the presence of his Spirit leading me each day.

I remember several years ago a Sunday that I was visiting Ginghamsburg Church near Dayton, Ohio. I thought I was there as an observer, but I quickly became an active worshiper. Pastor Mike Slaughter was preaching this message: Some of us have had a conversion of the head. (We believe Jesus is the son of God. We believe he died for our sins. We believe he rose again from the dead…). Some of us have had a conversion of the hands. (We are committed to giving our money and time and talents to further God's mission.) But what God is calling us to is a conversion of the heart. I knew that those words were spoken for me, and to me. There was a reason I was there at that particular worship service. And I heard Jesus asking me for a conversion of my heart. What Jesus wants from me is what he wanted from Peter. "Peter, do you love me?" (John 21:15)

More than our acceptance, our commitment, and our service, Jesus wants our love. He invites us to know him, to belong to him, and to love him. To move beyond belief to experience, beyond propositions to a relationship of love. I pray that I may love God in such a way that I may hold nothing back.

Questions for reflection

Sometimes faith of the head is contrasted to faith of the heart. What do you think…is one better than the other? Are both important? Where do you fall on the head – heart spectrum?

I do not know. I do not understand how these two things work.

I challenge that there is such simplicity rather than rich complexity.

Why does Jesus ask Peter the same question (do you love me?) three times? How many times does he ask this question of you?

3x

3 seasons of life and calling I think.

Many speak of how it serves Peter, reinstates, affirms in correlation to his denials. But I deny Christ far more often. Perhaps it is more Christ speaking into being these seasons, more truth/fact, than else.

What does it look like to love the Lord your God with all your heart, mind, soul, and strength?

to be Christ - to perfectly fulfill the law. For me it is to have faith that Christ has done this for me.

Prayer: *"Gracious and holy God, give us diligence to seek you, wisdom to perceive you, and patience to wait for you. Grant us, O God, a mind to meditate on you; eyes to behold you; ears to listen for your word; a heart to love you; and a life to proclaim you; through the power of the Spirit of Jesus Christ, our Savior and Lord. Amen."*[14]

Day 6: The Real Hunger

> ***Matthew 6:25-30*** *"Therefore I tell you, do not worry about your life, what you will eat or what you will drink, or about your body, what you will wear. Is not life more than food, and the body more than clothing? [26]Look at the birds of the air; they neither sow nor reap nor gather into barns, and yet your heavenly Father feeds them. Are you not of more value than they? [27]And can any of you by worrying add a single hour to your span of life? [28]And why do you worry about clothing? Consider the lilies of the field, how they grow; they neither toil nor spin, [29]yet I tell you, even Solomon in all his glory was not clothed like one of these. [30]But if God so clothes the grass of the field, which is alive today and tomorrow is thrown into the oven, will he not much more clothe you – you of little faith?*

In his book, *Following Jesus through the Eye of a Needle*, Kent Annan the author discusses his ministry with Beyond Borders in Haiti. He writes, "Part of why I looked forward to moving to Haiti is because I hate how easy it is to satiate my hunger for God and for good and for love by stuffing my appetites with food, with entertainment, with ambition, with stuff. How easy it is to fill the echo chamber that calls me toward God and good and love with other clanging noises. The absence in Haiti of choices to feed this profound hunger is unpleasant…but I need it. I'm too often too weak to hunger for good (or, to be more biblical, to seek the kingdom of God) and to pull away from the dancing lights that have embarrassing power over me, like over a mindless, fluttering moth."[15]

When we're seeking something else foremost in our lives other than God and God's purpose for us, we will struggle with anxiety. That's why Jesus tells us: seek first and foremost God's kingdom, and the rest of your things will fall into their proper places.

The hunger for God that Kent Annan speaks of often leads to a deep restlessness or anxiety. We have been discussing how that hunger for God is so persistent, so deep-seated in us, that we seek out many things to try to fill it. We try to find our own validation, our own sense of worth or connectedness in our own ways and by our own means. As the song says, we end up looking for love in all the wrong places. And therefore hearts are empty, and lives are unfulfilled.

We think we can make our own life's meaning. When all along, all we have to do is look at the birds and the lilies, all of creation, in fact, to see the signs of God's deep love for us (Matthew 6:25-30). Or we can look at the cross, and be reminded of the extent God would go to reconcile the world to himself. Or we can receive the bread and wine, the body and blood of Jesus Christ, to receive and taste that love.

"Little faiths," Jesus says, let tomorrow take care of tomorrow. What you have is today. And what you have today is everything you need, what your heart hungers for. Because you have God the Father, and God the Father has you. (Matthew 6:30-33)

Questions for reflection:

What are we supposed to learn from the lilies and birds (Matthew 6:25-34)?

God's provision, our needs, faithful dependence and even as Job, God's sovereignty.

In what other ways do you see God's love for you?

His patience with me.

Prayer: *It is true, Lord. You have given me today. You have given me all I need…even Yourself. I thank you will all my heart. Amen.*

Taking It Further: Small Group and Chapter Summary Questions

Discuss how the yearning for meaning and the yearning for connection (relationship) both lead us to God.

the two are so closely connected. Both seem inherent, natural, present in all people. And both seem neverending; both seem to only find glimmers of fulfillment in God alone.

Deb Meyers (Day 2) offers us a promise that we need to hear again and again: "God tells us that we are loved with His unfailing love; that we are accepted, chosen, forgiven, and redeemed. He is our rock-- the one we can cling to, the one we can count on, the one who loves us and says he will never let us go." How do you respond to that promise?

Why is this so hard to hear, know, experience?, believe, trust?

Why is this the place of such central brokenness — ~~untrust was~~ a lack of trust between myself and my Creator?

Why must we wrestle so and toil in this perpetual state of brokenness — oh how I yearn for the day when such things will not even be a distant memory.

How was your relationship to God deepened this week?

Has it? What does "deeper" even mean?

I find that He has helped me see the gap between my present and my aspirations.

I think he wants me to see how to lean into closing those gaps. I do not know the line of participation and active verse passive — my theology seem less clear and more meaning is found in its ambiguity lately — but He is God and so I trust Him.

Perhaps this means our relationship is deeper?

What questions or issues would you like to discuss with others?

Why am I arrogant so quickly and easily?

Why do so many people have such limited ability and spiritual maturity?

Which of the Bible readings took on a new meaning for you this week?

?

I think God worked more through prayer this week and gave me a big gift: "close the gap."

I remain tethered to Scripture, but sometimes God uses things alongside Scripture.

What do you want to remember from this chapter?

the depth to which all people yearn for connection

"Close the gap"

Recommended resources for further study:

M. Craig Barnes, *Yearning: Living Between How It Is & How It Ought To Be*

Brian McLaren, *Finding Faith: A Search for What Is Real*

Brian McLaren, *Finding Faith: A Search for What Makes Sense*

Henri Nouwen, *A Cry For Mercy: Prayers from the Genesee*

James Bryan Smith, *Embracing the Love of God: The Path and Promise of Christian Life*

Chapter Three: Life-Changing Encounters with Jesus

Meeting Jesus

Richard Foster writes that the recurring message of God in the Bible is: "'I am with you – will you be with Me?' Every story in the Bible, no matter its twists and turns, whether the human characters are trustworthy or untrustworthy, whether the story is sad or happy, is built on this clarion call to relationship.'I am with you – will you be with me?'"[16]

"From Genesis to Revelation, throughout human history, the Bible tells the stories of people learning to turn back to God. Always, it is God's grace and power drawing them and supporting them, giving them the means to become transformed into the kind of people who will gladly and freely choose life in the eternally loving community of God's People. God wants relationship with us, not mechanical transactions. And so he teaches us through the flesh and blood of ordinary people whose wayward steps were straightened and made firm by the power of God at work among them."[17]

Ultimately in Jesus of Nazareth God's message (God's Word) becomes most clear. It all comes down to Jesus. "There was nothing normal about him, and everything normal about him. He fit in effortlessly yet stood out magnificently. He was a living paradox. When Jesus was born, the eternal became temporary. The king of all became the slave of everyone. The light of life entered the valley of the shadow of death and transformed it forever."[18]

Day 1: Good News

> ***Matthew 5:3-6*** *"Blessed are the poor in spirit, for theirs is the kingdom of heaven. [4]"Blessed are those who mourn, for they will be comforted. [5]"Blessed are the meek, for they will inherit the earth. [6]"Blessed are those who hunger and thirst for righteousness, for they will be filled.*

Jesus announced that the kingdom of God (or "the age to come," or "the time of God's favor") had arrived. He pronounced blessing on those who were not considered blessed (the poor in spirit, the meek, the sorrowful, and those under the weight of injustice – Matthew 5:3-6). Jesus said that he came for sinners, and he was often seen associating with outcasts and disreputable people. All were invited to the party of God's reign, even gentiles and tax collectors, and many others who were usually omitted from the religious rites. ("Go out at once into the streets and lanes of the town and bring in the poor, the crippled, the blind, and the lame." Luke 14:21) Crowds of people followed Jesus because they heard from him and saw in him good news.

Imagine for a moment if we were able to ask the first followers of Jesus how Jesus was good news in their lives…what might they have said?

Peter, what is the good news of Jesus for you?
"The Lord forgave even my betrayal of him."

Thomas, what about you?
"Jesus was patient with my doubts and showed me that he has conquered death."

Matthew, how was Jesus good news for you?
"Jesus loved me when nobody else did, and he gave me a new start."

Mary of Bethany, what about you?
"Jesus taught me as a disciple, even though I am a woman."

What would you say, **Bartimaeus**?
"He noticed me, he called me, he gave me my sight and let me follow him."

Zacchaeus, what about you?
"He said that in spite of all I'd ever done, I could still be a part of God's great plan for the world."[19]

Each was met by Jesus and changed forever. Jesus met them as individuals and was good news to them in unique ways.

The good news is that Jesus continues to meet us in our own need. Norma Cook Everist puts it this way: "If the human problem is brokenness, the good news is that Jesus makes us whole. If the human problem is alienation, the good news is God reconciles and restores relationships. If the human problem is guilt, the good news is God through Jesus Christ forgives. If the human problem is being lost, the good news is that the Good Shepherd looks for and finds the lost. If the human problem is death, the good news is Jesus Christ has brought new life. If the human problem is judgment, the good news is that in Jesus Christ there is unconditional acceptance. If the human problem is bondage, the good news is that Jesus brings freedom."[20]

Question for reflection:

What is the good news/gospel for you? (In what ways has Jesus been good news in your life?)

He loves me even as I struggle to love myself.

Prayer: *Lord of all, you not only bring good news to the world – you are the good news for us all. Thank you for your deep love for the world and for me. Amen.*

Day 2: Jesus Is the Good News

Jesus not only proclaimed the good news, he himself was (and is) the good news. God's love for the world was most evident in his person. The gospel (good news) is about Jesus Christ.

The message of the Bible can be summarized as "a world full of people who insist on going their own way and a God who relentlessly pursues them."[21]

One of the primary beliefs of the Christian Church, and one of its primary motivations for mission is the belief that people need Jesus Christ. When we talk about why people need Jesus Christ, we are talking about the gospel or the good news about Jesus. Authors Bliese and Van Gelder offer this definition: The gospel is the good news of a God, who through the cross and resurrection of Jesus Christ, calls us out of "an old life of darkness and death and into a new life of purpose and hope and uncontainable joy."[22]

Right away we see that when we define the gospel (the good news), there needs to be a corresponding description of the human condition (the bad news). That is, there is something about the human condition that needs restoring, correcting, or resolving. (Lutherans would say that this is the message of "the law," that we are sinful creatures, and there is nothing we can do to rectify that or to earn God's favor.)

We use the word "sin" to describe this human condition. In the Bible, sin is described as disobedience or unfaithfulness to God. It has also been described by theologians as estrangement from God, as a separation from the one to whom we belong (Tillich). Some theologians have written that the root sin is pride--Niebuhr/Augustine--or self-centeredness. "Sin is thinking our lives belong to us, to live as we see fit, thinking that the world is our own to make use of in whatever way we like. Sin is the state of the world that organizes itself as though God were irrelevant."[23]

Sin is not the only biblical image for the problem of the human condition. Here are some other images or metaphors:

> blindness (humans are blind and cannot see their way);
> in exile (humans are in exile and are longing for home);
> in bondage (humans are in bondage and longing to be free);
> closed hearts or hard hearts (humans have closed hearts or are in need of new hearts);
> hunger and thirst (humans are hungering and thirsting for that which can satisfy);
> lost (humans are lost and needing to be found);
> dead (humans are dry bones, cut off from the land of the living).[24]

With those descriptions of the problem of the human condition, we can now appreciate the rationale behind the many names and titles for Jesus in the New Testament:

> Jesus is the Lamb of God who takes away the sin of the world. (John 1:29)
> Jesus is the Savior of the world. (I John 4:14)
> Jesus is the light of the world. (John 9:5; Jesus makes the blind see.)
> Jesus is "the way" home to God. (John 14:6)
> Jesus is the healer; he heals people of their infirmities and releases them from bondage to evil. (Mark 1:32-34)
> Jesus himself is the new heart and new spirit in people. (Whoever is in Christ is a new person…2 Corinthians 5:17)

Jesus is the bread of life (who alone satisfies our hunger); (John 6:35)
Jesus is the living water (who alone quenches our thirst); (John 4:10; 7:37-38)
Jesus is the good shepherd in search of the lost sheep. (John 10:11)
Jesus is the resurrection and the life. (John 11:25-26)
Jesus brings peace and is our peace with God and one another. (Ephesians 2:13-14)

The Bible says it in so many ways. Jesus is God's self-revelation to humanity. Jesus brings about the reconciliation of humanity to God. Jesus is the answer to the human problem. Jesus is the fulfillment of the deepest longings of the human heart. It's all about Jesus: if there's no Jesus, there's no good news.

Questions for reflection:

What two or three statements or images about Jesus (above) best describe your current relationship to Jesus and his meaning to you? Form one of the statements into a prayer of thanks that you know Jesus in this way.

teacher - Rabonni - for my desire to learn and live right
ressurection and life - for my fear of death
leader - one I would follow - "the Way"
the "Word" as my defender, general of God's army/people
one who frees - sets the captive free from chains, cell, locks that bind

What is your experience of meeting Jesus? Has it been a long term journey or a sudden development?[25]

His presence and calling is persistant. I am one of the children a set of parents brought to him; I grew up knowing him, following him, listening to him. And I am grateful as I meet others and their stories - I am grateful to have known him for so long.

Day 3: Authority and Authenticity

> ***Matthew 7:28-29*** *Now when Jesus had finished saying these things, the crowds were astounded at his teaching, [29]for he taught them as one having authority, and not as their scribes.*

What was it about Jesus? What did people see in him? One word that the gospels use is "authority:" people noticed his authority. He taught with authority (Mark 1:22, 27). He spoke from a personal knowledge of God. His miracles and signs revealed an authority (the power of God) over other powers. He had power to heal. He had authority to forgive sins.

The people were amazed at the teaching of Jesus. There was something captivating about Jesus. He surrounded himself with the most unlikely people. He embodied and preached about the extravagant grace of God. Nobody else taught like he did. Nobody said the same kinds of things. Brilliant things. The Pharisees and scribes studied, interpreted and taught the scriptures too, but not with this kind of authority. He didn't water down the scriptures. He took them more seriously than they have ever been taken. He cut right to the heart of the matter. He looked deep into the human heart. And people knew he spoke the truth.[26]

People were also impressed with Jesus' authenticity. He lived his message, and because he lived it, his words were experienced as well as heard. When he spoke, people leaned in with anticipation. Jesus spoke and lived the truth. There was an exact integrity between what he taught and how he lived. Jesus didn't just teach the truth…he was the truth. Jesus didn't just point to the way…he was the way. Jesus didn't just offer life…he was the life.

In John 5:39-40, Jesus says, "You search the scriptures because you think that in them you have eternal life; and it is they that testify on my behalf. Yet you refuse to come to me to have life."

Many did not know what to make of Jesus. "Some thought he was a dangerous terrorist (John 11:48; Luke 23:14). Others said he was possessed by demons (Matthew 9:34). His own family thought he was certifiably crazy (Mark 3:21). A few people believed he was actually the long-awaited, one and only Savior of the human race (Matthew 16:16; Acts 4:12)."[27]

In the gospel stories, it is those who are most aware of their own need for rescue that are the most welcoming of Jesus. "People who saw themselves as spiritually 'together,' however, felt deeply threatened by Jesus."[28]

Questions for reflection:

Which impresses you more, Jesus' authority or his authenticity? Which do you desire more in your own life?

How can I say one more than another.

Why were the religious people most threatened by Jesus?

He challenged what they thought they knew; he was so penetrating.

He was not always clear; he was not always pointed; he was not always challenging. But he did seem always profound, impactful, important, penetrating.

We religious people build so much upon our convictions. We draw so confidently - arrogantly at times - desperately always in order to remain sane.

Prayer: *Lord, grow within us the desire to immerse ourselves in the scriptures so that we may know more deeply who you are. Amen.*

Day 4: Reactions to Jesus

Jesus proclaimed that God's kingdom has arrived and all were invited into God's mission to restore the world.

Some people followed Jesus, seemingly on the spot, leaving family and occupations:

As he walked by the Sea of Galilee, he saw two brothers, Simon, who is called Peter, and Andrew his brother, casting a net into the sea-- for they were fishermen. [19]And he said to them, "Follow me, and I will make you fish for people." [20]Immediately they left their nets and followed him. [21]As he went from there, he saw two other brothers, James son of Zebedee and his brother John, in the boat with their father Zebedee, mending their nets, and he called them. [22]Immediately they left the boat and their father, and followed him. ***(Matthew 4:18-22).***

Others were reluctant or had questions:

Nicodemus - *"How can anyone be born after having grown old? Can one enter a second time into the mother's womb and be born?" (John 3:4) "How can these things be?"* ***(John 3:9)***

Nathanael - *"Can anything good come out of Nazareth?"* ***(John 1:46)***

John the Baptist - *"Are you the one who is to come, or are we to wait for another?"* ***(Matthew 11:3)***

Some tried to change the subject when Jesus got too close to the truth:

Samaritan woman - *"Sir, I see that you are a prophet. [20]Our ancestors worshiped on this mountain, but you say that the place where people must worship is in Jerusalem."* ***(John 4:19-20)***

Others were preoccupied with other matters:

"Lord, first let me go and bury my father." ***(Luke 9:59)***

"I will follow you, Lord; but let me first say farewell to those at my home." ***(Luke 9:61)***

For some the call of Jesus to follow was too demanding:

When he heard this, he was shocked and went away grieving, for he had many possessions. ***(Mark 10:22)***

Because of this many of his disciples turned back and no longer went about with him. [67]So Jesus asked the twelve, "Do you also wish to go away?" ***(John 6:66-67)***

For others, like Zacchaeus, meeting Jesus opens up a whole new world and a new life. When they find Jesus or are found by him, many realize that he is what they've wanted all along:

Zacchaeus stood there and said to the Lord, "Look, half of my possessions, Lord, I will give to the poor; and if I have defrauded anyone of anything, I will pay back four times as much." [9] Then Jesus said to him, "Today salvation has come to this house, because he too is a son of Abraham. ***(Luke 19:8-9)***

In the following chapters, as we take an in-depth look at the life stories of several followers of Jesus (as well as some who did not follow Jesus), we will see how after they met Jesus, they were never the same. Their lives were changed forever.[29]

Questions for reflection:

When have you heard Jesus calling you to follow him?

there have been pivotal moments in life
in highschool, college, seminary

Which reaction to Jesus (discussed above) best describes your response to Jesus' call?

the disciples - I just did, almost compelled
by that call.

What have you learned about Jesus as you have followed him?

that I know so little, and there is much
yet to learn and do as I follow Him

What have you learned about yourself as you have followed Jesus? (Offer those "learnings" to God in prayer.)

I am loved.

I can.

I can and can't, am paradox.

I know so little and am so small.

Day 5: A Heart for Christ above All Else

When Jesus calls someone to follow, he expects a full devotion to himself.

Jesus tells his followers, "I've come to change everything, turn everything right-side up – how I long for it to be finished! Do you think I came to smooth things over and make everything nice? Not so. I've come to disrupt and confront! From now on, when you find five in a house, it will be – three against two and two against three." **(Luke 12:50-53; *Message*)**

Jesus is talking about the divisions that occur between people, between family members, between parents and children, husbands and wives, brothers and sisters, when Jesus walks into their lives. "He is talking about what happens to family loyalty when he asks them to put God first in their lives. He is talking about what happens to family harmony when he asks them to choose whom they will follow."[30]

What has been your own experience with friends and family as you have sought to follow Jesus?

> ***Mark 8:34-35*** *He called the crowd with his disciples, and said to them, "If any want to become my followers, let them deny themselves and take up their cross and follow me. 35 For those who want to save their life will lose it, and those who lose their life for my sake, and for the sake of the gospel, will save it.*

A kind of death is involved in following Jesus, a death of self and self-will, and a taking up of Jesus' agenda. (Bonhoeffer writes that when Jesus calls a person, he calls that person to come and die.[31])

> ***Luke 9:57-62*** *As they were going along the road, someone said to him, "I will follow you wherever you go." 58And Jesus said to him, "Foxes have holes, and birds of the air have nests; but the Son of Man has nowhere to lay his head." 59To another he said, "Follow me." But he said, "Lord, first let me go and bury my father." 60But Jesus said to him, "Let the dead bury their own dead; but as for you, go and proclaim the kingdom of God." 61Another said, "I will follow you, Lord; but let me first say farewell to those at my home." 62Jesus said to him, "No one who puts a hand to the plow and looks back is fit for the kingdom of God."*

When Jesus calls people to follow, he expects a complete commitment. In Luke 9, Jesus responds to the would-be follower who wanted to fulfill family obligations to bury his father: "Let the dead bury the dead." To the one who wanted to go home and say farewell to his family, Jesus replies: "No one who puts a hand to the plow and looks back is fit for the kingdom of God." Jesus challenges the rich young man who wanted more in life, "Go sell all your possessions and give the money to the poor, and then come and follow me."

In these very challenging statements, Jesus says that "loyalty to God is not one allegiance to be juggled along with all the rest. It is primary. It is not negotiable. It is a matter of life and death, although sometimes you have to be on the road to Jerusalem before you can see it that way."[32] Jesus expects our highest devotion. "Do you think I came to smooth things over and make everything nice? Not so. I've come to disrupt and confront!" (Luke 12:51, *Message*)

Questions for reflection:

What do you think Jesus meant when he said, "Do you think that I have come to bring peace to the earth? No, I tell you, but rather division!" (Luke 12:51; compare Matthew 10:34)

Christ divides good and evil, he confronts ~~of~~ our shortcomings and calls things what they are.

Does that sound like the Jesus you know? Why or why not?

Yes. As graceful as He is, he first demands a death of the old self to let the new one live

Why does Jesus seem to have such a sense of urgency for people to respond?

Because everyday lived outside his Way leads to death, destruction and heart ache. So all who have ears let him hear.

Prayer: *Sometimes I wonder, Lord, if I will ever be able to make you my primary loyalty. It will only happen through your grace in my life. May I give up my control; may I step over the line; may I hold nothing back. Amen.*

Day 6: Where Else Would I Go?

In John's gospel, as he taught and traveled, Jesus was drawing large crowds. Some came to see Jesus because they were curious about him. Others wanted something from him, a healing for example. Others felt threatened by Jesus and they were looking to trip him in his words or find fault with his actions. Others thought he had special potential to set his people free from Roman rule.

In John 6, Jesus feeds a crowd of several thousand with a few loaves and fish. When the people saw the sign that he had done, they began to say, "This is indeed the prophet who is to come into the world." They wanted to take him right there and make Jesus their king, but he withdrew to the mountains to be by himself. (John 6:14-15)

They called Jesus a prophet, and that was true, but he was much more than a prophet. They wanted to make him their king, and it was true he was the Messiah, God's anointed king, but he was much more than a king/Messiah.

Jesus called himself the "bread of God" that comes down from heaven and gives life to the world. He said: "I am the bread of life. Whoever comes to me will never be hungry, and whoever believes in me will never be thirsty." (John 6:33-35) "Whoever eats of this bread will live forever; and the bread that I will give for the life of the world is my flesh." (6:51) "Those who eat my flesh and drink my blood abide in me, and I in them." (6:56)

When many of his disciples heard these sayings of Jesus, they said, "This teaching is difficult; who can accept it?" Because of these teachings, many of the disciples of Jesus turned back and no longer went about with him. Jesus, it seems, had gone too far.

Some disciples stopped following Jesus because they could not understand his teachings. But other disciples stopped following Jesus because they understood all too well what Jesus was saying. They began to realize what Jesus meant when he said he would give his flesh and blood for the life of the world. And they understood that he was calling his followers to give their lives away, to be bread broken and wine poured out for the world. They thought Jesus was asking too much, so they walked away from Jesus and followed him no more.

At least the twelve disciples, his closest companions, remained with Jesus, and Jesus turned to them and asked: "Do you also wish to go away?" I wonder, did he ask that to challenge them? Or did he ask it out of sadness and discouragement? Do you also wish to go away? (6:67)

I love Peter's response: "Lord, to whom can we go? You have the words of eternal life. We have come to believe and know that you are the Holy One of God." (Our gospel acclamation.)

Do you also wish to go away? Maybe you've asked yourself that question. Maybe the doubts or questions or troubles or pains in your life are that large.

The way I see it is that we will always have questions and hurts in our lives. But finally they do not negate the significance of Jesus in our lives. Do you also wish to go away? As for me, I answer the question as Peter does: Where else would I go? You have the words of grace and forgiveness. Where else would I go? You have the words of healing and deliverance. Where else would I go? You have the words of renewal and real life. Where else would I go? You give us the best possible life, life in all its fullness.

I may not be able to answer all the questions about my faith, or about God, or about life, but I've seen how God has blessed me, and what he has done for me. I've come to know the transforming power of God's love. I know that God's grace is more than sufficient. I know that Jesus is the embodiment of peace and goodness and truth and love, that Jesus is God himself. And in the deepest part of me, I know Jesus satisfies my hunger and quenches my thirst like nothing else can. Where else would I go?

Questions for reflection:

Do you remember times when you wanted to walk away (or you did walk away) because following Jesus was too challenging? What were they?

the moments of temptation, deep comparison – where abandoning faith "looks" like it is rewarding... but truly, to where would we go? The words are true. This world and life is hollow apart from Christ. This I know and beleive to be true.

Would you rather be seen as a normal person or a "Jesus freak"? Why?

My heart is to be faithful, regardless of whether that makes me normal or a freak.

What if one of the meanings of the Eucharist (communion), or one of the ways we share communion "in remembrance" of Jesus, is by lives broken and poured out for the world? What are your reactions to that thought?

In as much as we conform to the likeness of Christ, our lives will be broken and poured out for others.

Prayer: *Lord, where else would I go? You have the words of eternal life. I have come to believe and know that you are the Holy One of God. Amen.*

Alleluia refrain

Taking It Further: Small Group and Chapter Summary Questions

What does this statement mean to you: Jesus is the lens through which I see God?

Richard Foster summarizes God's message as: "I am with you – will you be with me?" Where do you hear that message most clearly in scripture?

What is most challenging about Jesus' call for you to follow him?

What questions or issues would you like to discuss with others?

Which of the Bible readings took on a new meaning for you this week?

How was your relationship to God deepened this week?

What do you want to remember from this chapter?

Recommended resources for further study:

Dietrich Bonhoeffer, *The Cost of Discipleship*

Chapter Four: Born Anew

A man named Nicodemus, a member of the Sanhedrin, comes to Jesus at night. This is a man of means and authority, sitting on the highest Jewish council, one of 70 leaders, governing the affairs of the Jewish people. This respectable leader wants to meet Jesus. He says to Jesus, "Rabbi, we know that you are a teacher that has come from God; for no one can do these signs that you do apart from the presence of God."

Nicodemus comes to Jesus at night, not wanting to be seen by others. Perhaps he doesn't want the conversation to be overheard. Evidently there is a risk for someone on the Sanhedrin to show interest in this itinerant rabbi, Jesus. Perhaps he has some personal questions that he wants Jesus to answer. Perhaps he recognizes that something is missing in his life? Perhaps he longs for something more? Perhaps he sees that something more in Jesus? "Rabbi, he says, I know that you are from God. God's presence is with you."

Rather than saying, "Why, thank you, Nicodemus, that's very kind," Jesus pushes back at Nicodemus and invites him to take a life-changing step. "Very truly, I tell you, no one can see the kingdom of God without being born from above." This is a man whom we would think had it all figured out, and Jesus invites him to start over. Nicodemus had the entire scriptures memorized. He could tell you all 613 commandments. Jesus tells him he has to start anew. No one can enter God's kingdom without being born from above.[33]

Nicodemus appears to misunderstand this birth metaphor, so he asks Jesus to explain. Jesus adds another metaphor. "Very truly, I tell you, no one can enter the kingdom of God without being born of water and Spirit." (John 3:5) Mention of the Spirit then leads Jesus to talk about the wind, and how you hear it and see its effect, but you cannot control it; you don't know where it comes from or where it's going. "So it is with everyone who is born of the Spirit."

Here is Nicodemus, so well versed in the law of the scriptures. He had invested his life in understanding the law and focusing on the actions the law requires. And here is Jesus, inviting Nicodemus into a whole new orientation, a new life, a new righteousness, a new heart. It's not about religion, Nicodemus; it's about relationship. This new life is "given of God, from above, unearned, and unachieved. Being from above, the life eternal is uncontrolled, uncharted, and uncalculated. It is as mysterious as the whence and whither of the wind."[34]

Nicodemus took a risk. He acknowledged that he didn't have it all figured out. He "let go of familiar controls, and allowed the wind of God to bear him to Jesus. Jesus invites him to let go still further, to yield to the birthing breath of God."[35] It's too much for Nicodemus at that moment. All he can say is, "How can these things be?" He comes to Jesus to discuss some things. And Jesus invites him to step into a whole new life. Nicodemus was looking to discuss; he was not prepared to surrender.

> ***John 3:1-21*** *Now there was a Pharisee named Nicodemus, a leader of the Jews.* [2]*He came to Jesus by night and said to him, "Rabbi, we know that you are a teacher who has come from God; for no one can do these signs that you do apart from the*

presence of God." [3]Jesus answered him, "Very truly, I tell you, no one can see the kingdom of God without being born from above." [4]Nicodemus said to him, "How can anyone be born after having grown old? Can one enter a second time into the mother's womb and be born?" [5]Jesus answered, "Very truly, I tell you, no one can enter the kingdom of God without being born of water and Spirit. [6]What is born of the flesh is flesh, and what is born of the Spirit is spirit. [7]Do not be astonished that I said to you, 'You must be born from above.' [8]The wind blows where it chooses, and you hear the sound of it, but you do not know where it comes from or where it goes. So it is with everyone who is born of the Spirit." [9]Nicodemus said to him, "How can these things be?" [10]Jesus answered him, "Are you a teacher of Israel, and yet you do not understand these things? [11]"Very truly, I tell you, we speak of what we know and testify to what we have seen; yet you do not receive our testimony. [12]If I have told you about earthly things and you do not believe, how can you believe if I tell you about heavenly things? [13]No one has ascended into heaven except the one who descended from heaven, the Son of Man. [14] And just as Moses lifted up the serpent in the wilderness, so must the Son of Man be lifted up, [15]that whoever believes in him may have eternal life. [16]"For God so loved the world that he gave his only Son, so that everyone who believes in him may not perish but may have eternal life. [17]"Indeed, God did not send the Son into the world to condemn the world, but in order that the world might be saved through him. [18]Those who believe in him are not condemned; but those who do not believe are condemned already, because they have not believed in the name of the only Son of God. [19]And this is the judgment, that the light has come into the world, and people loved darkness rather than light because their deeds were evil. [20]For all who do evil hate the light and do not come to the light, so that their deeds may not be exposed. [21]But those who do what is true come to the light, so that it may be clearly seen that their deeds have been done in God."

Day 1: Encountering Truth (Jane Norris)

John 3:1-17 (above)

Nicodemus sneaks out in the middle of the night to speak to Jesus. No doubt he prayed that no one would see him. What in the world would people think if they saw him talking to that radical rabbi? Nicodemus, a Pharisee, is a member of the Sanhedrin, a defender of the law with a zealous image and spotless reputation to uphold. Even Jesus calls him "Israel's teacher." But being seen with Him is too big a risk.

Maybe Jesus' teachings have rattled Nicodemus out of believing he has all the answers. Maybe he can get a better grip on the words that have shaken up his world by asking Jesus privately, where his colleagues won't get the wrong idea. But if he's seeking safe, tidy, legalistic explanations and a comfortable excuse to slip back into the status quo, it's too late. Everything he thought he knew has been turned upside down. Something has ignited within him that a sound bite can't extinguish, and there's no going back.

Somehow, deep inside, Nicodemus has recognized who Jesus really is. Nothing in his scholarly background has prepared him for this moment. He doesn't have a clue yet that what he's feeling is the Spirit's beckoning, and that it can lead him to all the answers he seeks.

Nicodemus is getting his first inkling that the Holy Spirit can be a personal, internal force for change that can accomplish what decades of toeing the line, maintaining facades and keeping up with the Joneses can't deliver. That it's never too late to try again. That everyone deserves a divine do-over. That the Spirit can lead us home to our individual answers to the eternal "Now what do I do?" Nicodemus almost gets his wish to get away unseen; he's mentioned only in the Gospel of John, and then only three times. He is an excellent guide for us today in our self-conscious but rarely self-aware society. He taps right into two of our deepest human questions: Would we recognize the truth if we heard it? And, if we did, how would we know what to do with it?

His brief but powerful story examines the selves we want people to see, the selves we'd die before we'd let others see and the God who's willing to die to teach us that our true selves are the only ones that matter, and the ones He dearly loves.

Questions for reflection:

You may come away with more questions than answers this week, but don't worry. As we follow Nicodemus, pausing at the three distinct landmarks we know of his journey, keep in mind the promises of Isaiah 43:18-19 and 2 Corinthians 5:17. God is doing something new here. Can Nicodemus perceive it? Can we?

I don't get this one

Isaiah 43:18-19 - *Do not remember the former things, or consider the things of old. I am about to do a new thing; now it springs forth, do you not perceive it? I will make a way in the wilderness and rivers in the desert.*

2 Corinthians 5:17 - *So if anyone is in Christ, there is a new creation: everything old has passed away; see, everything has become new!*

What new (or unexpected) things have you seen God work in your own life? (Offer a prayer of thanksgiving for God's work in your life.)

Have you had a life event which turned your life upside down? What happened? How do you view it now?

Day 2: Encountering Rebirth (Jane Norris)

> ***John 3:14-15*** *And just as Moses lifted up the serpent in the wilderness, so must the Son of Man be lifted up, [15]that whoever believes in him may have eternal life.*
>
> ***Numbers 21:7-9*** *The people came to Moses and said, "We have sinned by speaking against the LORD and against you; pray to the LORD to take away the serpents from us." So Moses prayed for the people. [8]And the LORD said to Moses, "Make a poisonous serpent, and set it on a pole; and everyone who is bitten shall look at it and live." [9]So Moses made a serpent of bronze, and put it upon a pole; and whenever a serpent bit someone, that person would look at the serpent of bronze and live.*

Sometimes, when God is doing something new, the symbols we see every day take on entirely different meanings. Jesus reminds Nicodemus of the time when Moses asked God to protect the people from venomous snakes in the wilderness. God told Moses to make a snake out of bronze, fasten it to a pole and lift it where everyone can see it. Anyone who trusted Him, followed His instructions and looked up at the snake escaped an agonizing death by neurotoxin.

God was reminding Moses and the people to look up for their help and salvation instead of down. He got their attention by taking a symbol that made people uncomfortable and turning it into a sign of new hope. In the Old Testament, He selected a snake. In the New Testament, He chose a cross.

The serpent is a painfully squirmy reminder of lost Eden and the first time people muted their consciences to indulge selfish impulses. The cross made people equally uncomfortable. The image of the cross repulsed the people of Nicodemus' time; perhaps it was similar to the way looking at a gas chamber or a lethal-injection gurney would feel today.

But snakes offer us another lesson we can take to heart while we grow along with Nicodemus. Snakes shed their skins periodically so they can grow. The scaly outer sheath that has outlived its usefulness gradually splits, shreds and falls away. The renewed snake that emerges is supple, flexible and ready for a fresh start.

Wriggling out of old attitudes, labels and paradigms we've outgrown and leaving them behind can be intensely difficult, but it can be equally liberating. We can't look down at the shreds of our old lives to be saved. We have to look up at the cross. If we scurry back to the safety of the darkness, we'll never get the chance to grow in the warmth of the light. Snakes shrug off the outgrown bindings that no longer serve them. Can Nicodemus? Can we?

Questions for reflection:

In Philippians 3:3-12, Paul counts his religious credentials as garbage, that he may trust in and know Jesus Christ and the power of his resurrection. How does that relate to Jesus' conversation with Nicodemus?

the Sanhedrin, and perhaps we in our own way, define life specifically and with established norms as created by a broken human system.

Christ challenges this.

Do you see any nuances or distinctions in the translations, being "born anew," being "born again," and being "born from above?" Do you have a preference?

a new – the others have dispositions but born a new is the most profound to me.

How does (your) baptism lead to a new birth?

My baptism, that adoption, is when life really began anew under God's rule and reign.

Prayer: *"O God, our leader and guide, in the waters of baptism your bring us to new birth to live as your children. Strengthen our faith in your promises, that by your Spirit we may lift up your life to all the world through your Son, Jesus Christ, our Savior and Lord." Amen.*[36]

Day 3: Encountering Spirit (Jane Norris)

> ***John 3:8*** *The wind blows where it chooses, and you hear the sound of it, but you do not know where it comes from or where it goes. So it is with everyone who is born of the Spirit.*
>
> ***Romans 8:26*** *- Likewise the Spirit helps us in our weakness; for we do not know how to pray as we ought, but that very Spirit intercedes with sighs too deep for words.*

I wasn't afraid of the wind when I was a child. That didn't happen until I bought a house. I can't remember sleeping through a single storm since I signed the papers. Since then, every wind advisory has sent my nervous imagination into overdrive. I can't help wondering if all the shingles might peel off the roof, or if the massive sycamore tree on the property line is planning to relocate to Orange County. Those are the times when I really need to read this verse again and get over myself.

Stumbling my way through John 3:8 showed me an oddly comforting parallel between the unnerving, invisible force that rattles my windows outside and the spontaneous, serendipitous movements of the Spirit inside that give my knuckle-white heart glimpses of a better way to live.

Thanks to the perfect storm of a naturally anxious personality, widowhood's unspoken sense of abandonment, more stress than sleep and far more work than play, I've practically turned into Piglet. I've turned hilariously irrational fears into an art form. But I don't have to keep living that way – not when I can turn inward and listen. Not when I can be still and know.

They're called "winds of change" for a reason. I must let His winds rip away my perfectionism, my pride and my last pointless resistance to the future that I will be given instead of the one that I'd planned for myself. I am a new creation, so I must stop being afraid of changes that could revitalize me and be gentler with myself when I don't get things right the first time.

The wind blows wherever it pleases, and I must keep my heart light enough to float along with it. I can't hide under the covers during life's storms and choose the darkness now that I know that the light is in the world.

It's all still a work in progress, so when misplaced ocean breath bears down on my beloved little house, I have no clue exactly what to pray for. But when I can't come up with the right words, the Spirit knows just what to say. With Him inside my heart, my foundation is secure. The same Spirit that shook up Nicodemus so profoundly the day he spoke with Jesus never left his heart, never left his side, never left him stranded. And He'd never leave me. No matter what happens, I am loudly and fiercely loved.

And that's why a set of wind chimes jingles by my kitchen door. I'm learning to listen for the beauty in the wind, and for the voice of the One who reminds me not to be afraid of it.

Questions for reflection:

With the winds of change, anything can happen. Can you blame Nicodemus for his reticence? Who wants to be blown about by an uncontrollable wind? But what if the wind is the holy purpose and power of God? Have you experienced such a wind? Would you like to?

Is not this the role of faith?

The wind blows where it chooses, Jesus says. In other words, we are not in control. Following Jesus, we may be led into directions we would not choose. What is your experience with this?

the call is not one of control but obedience

Prayer: *Although it may disrupt the status quo in my life, blow the wind of your Spirit in my life, as you desire. Amen.*

Day 4: Encountering Transformation (Jane Norris)

John 7:50-52 *Nicodemus, who had gone to Jesus before, and who was one of them, asked, [51] "Our law does not judge people without first giving them a hearing to find out what they are doing, does it?" [52]They replied, "Surely you are not also from Galilee, are you? Search and you will see that no prophet is to arise from Galilee."*

Philippians 3:7-11 *Yet whatever gains I had, these I have come to regard as loss because of Christ. [8]More than that, I regard everything as loss because of the surpassing value of knowing Christ Jesus my Lord. For his sake I have suffered the loss of all things, and I regard them as rubbish, in order that I may gain Christ [9]and be found in him, not having a righteousness of my own that comes from the law, but one that comes through faith in Christ, the righteousness from God based on faith. [10]I want to know Christ and the power of his resurrection and the sharing of his sufferings by becoming like him in his death, [11]if somehow I may attain the resurrection from the dead.*

Nicodemus recognizes that something profound and fundamental has shifted in his life since his late-night talk with Jesus, but he still has one foot in his old law-bound life and the other in the light of love. He's still Israel's teacher, still looked to as a keeper of the law.

So when Nicodemus asks the other leaders not to condemn Jesus without ascertaining the facts, his persuasiveness comes from his grounding in the law they say they defend. Listen to the way his colleagues respond: Name-calling. Denial. Labels. Label Nicodemus a Galilean like Jesus, and it's easier to tune him out. It's as if the leaders are twisting his words about Jesus to use against him. They're perfectly happy to condemn Jesus without listening to him, and they're about to do the same to Nicodemus.

They may never know that love is going to win the war with the law. They have no intention of leaving the darkness. Jesus would rather die than live without them, but they'd rather see Him dead and pretend that none of it ever happened.

The teacher has become a student. Nicodemus is realizing that he hasn't shed the constricting old skin of the law just to slither back under a rock of darkness. He won't even miss the shreds of whatever he leaves behind – reputation, career, intellectual identity – in the presence of what's far more important.

Questions for reflection:

Have you ever talked with another person who because he or she knew the "right answers" was not really able to enter into dialogue? Or have you ever caught yourself doing this?

Yes. It is hard and disheartening; it is one of my greatest temptations given my convictions.

It seems like Nicodemus had progressed along on his journey toward being born from above. What signs do you see that this may be the case?

He now challenges openly, but still...
Nicodemus like all disciples is more failure than success. His heart belongs to Christ yet still he argues based on law with lawmen.
In doing so, he is yet dependent upon the cross of Christ and a coming life.

Day 5: Encountering Resurrection (Jane Norris)

> ***John 19:38-41*** *After these things, Joseph of Arimathea, who was a disciple of Jesus, though a secret one because of his fear of the Jews, asked Pilate to let him take away the body of Jesus. Pilate gave him permission; so he came and removed his body.*
> *[39]Nicodemus, who had at first come to Jesus by night, also came, bringing a mixture of myrrh and aloes, weighing about a hundred pounds. [40]They took the body of Jesus and wrapped it with the spices in linen cloths, according to the burial custom of the Jews. [41]Now there was a garden in the place where he was crucified, and in the garden there was a new tomb in which no one had ever been laid.*

> ***John 3:20-21*** *For all who do evil hate the light and do not come to the light, so that their deeds may not be exposed. [31]But those who do what is true come to the light, so that it may be clearly seen that their deeds have been done in God."*

Perhaps being born again, born of the Spirit, means giving up the labels we wear like costumes and rejecting the labels we accept from others. Perhaps it means putting them all aside for a new identity that God longs to give us.

Sarai must have smiled when she stroked her newborn son's face and named him Isaac, because God indeed had had the last laugh. God had given his princess a precious new name – Sarah. Isaac soon would call her by the title she'd yearned for – Mother.

When Jesus beckoned, Levi left behind more than his label of tax collector and all the stereotypical resentment, envy and contempt it stirred in others. When he stepped into his new role as disciple, he didn't even take along his old name; we know him as Matthew.

After Jesus died on the cross, Joseph of Arimathea arrived to move His body to his own tomb. A secret disciple during Christ's life, Joseph had kept his devotion to Jesus hidden to protect his own reputation – but there he is, intentionally becoming unclean under the letter of the law by touching a dead body. A body taken down from a cross. On the eve of the Sabbath, no less. And who was his accomplice?

Who brought the traditional, expensive mix of fragrant myrrh and aloes to wrap into Jesus' grave clothes? Who helped Joseph bind up the body in accordance with the customs spelled out in the law? Who risked being seen in public in undeniable contact with the remains of the Galilean? Nicodemus.

This third and final time we see Nicodemus in the Bible, Israel's teacher is ritually unclean and linked in broad daylight to an executed criminal. He stands firmly outside the law that once defined him, and there's no turning back.

The wind blows wherever it pleases, just as Jesus told him. Nicodemus still has no idea where any of this is going. But at this solemn moment, in a way he never could have expected, Nicodemus is born again of the Spirit.

Questions for reflection:

Once again, Nicodemus comes to Jesus at night. This time he asks no questions. This time he carries the dead body of Jesus from the cross to its place of burial. Why, when all the other disciples had fled, would Nicodemus risk his own neck to bury the one who had invited him into a new life?

What if, as Nicodemus was carrying the body to its tomb, he was remembering what Jesus said about himself: "For God so loved the world that he gave his only Son, so that everyone who believes in him may not perish but may have eternal life?" What might those words have meant to him then?

it is a moment of fear, death, betrayal, hopelessness...

perhaps the question should be around Nicodemus on Easter...

Day 6: Faith

Nicodemus can only protest that he does not know what Jesus is talking about. Jesus responds, "If I have told you about earthly things and you do not believe, how can you believe if I tell you about heavenly things?' (John 3:12) Once again, as is typical in John's gospel, Jesus and a potential disciple are speaking on two different levels. There is water and there is Living Water. There is bread and there is the Bread of Life. There is the physical birth and there is the spiritual birth. In this conversation, there is belief and there is faith. What do you think is the difference between the two?

On one level, to believe someone means simply to accept what another person says is true. For example, someone tells you about, and even shows you a picture of himself climbing the rock face of a mountain, and you believe that that person has climbed and can climb mountains. "You accept the proposition. You give your intellectual assent, but it does not interfere with the way you live your life, because it is all in your head."[37]

There is another level of belief: faith. Instead of just showing you the pictures, your friend invites you to go rock climbing with him. As he helps you into your harness and runs your safety line through the D-ring around his own waist, he assures you that everything will be all right. You have now moved way past an intellectual assent, "I believe you," to a deep trust, "I believe in you." You are trusting him with your life.[38]

That is the journey to which Jesus invites Nicodemus. He thought he was coming at night to ask Jesus a few questions. But Jesus turns the table. "Believe in me. That was Jesus' dare to Nicodemus. Turn your mind inside out."[39] Ride the wind. Be born anew. Step from this solid ground to that little ledge, and lean into the rock-face. Believe in me. Trust me with your life. Trust me for your life.

Questions for reflection:

"For God so loved the world that he gave his only Son, so that everyone who believes in him may not perish but may have eternal life. Indeed, God did not send the Son into the world to condemn the world, but in order that the world might be saved through him." (John 3:16-17)

I beleive you vs I beleive in you

I have done this vs I have done this for you

What do those verses mean to you?

My life is so fortunate, yet when struggle comes I see & feel the difference in these statements. And the greatest struggle is our own mortality – death.

There at that moment may God grant me faith.

In what areas of your life is the wind blowing…is the Holy Spirit nudging you to change? Like Nicodemus, have you been reluctant to take the step? Do you hesitate to surrender? Ask God to show you the next steps to take.

Close the gap –

I see areas in my personal life –
working out ; QT ; rejuvenation

but I feel convoluted in my professional life

I think he is calling me to

teaching
culture
disipleship → leadership

Taking It Further: Small Group and Chapter Summary Questions

How do you connect (your) baptism to Jesus' conversation with Nicodemus?

Has the wind (the Holy Spirit) blown in your life in such a way that turned it upside down? What happened? How do you understand it now?

How are you/have you been similar to Nicodemus?

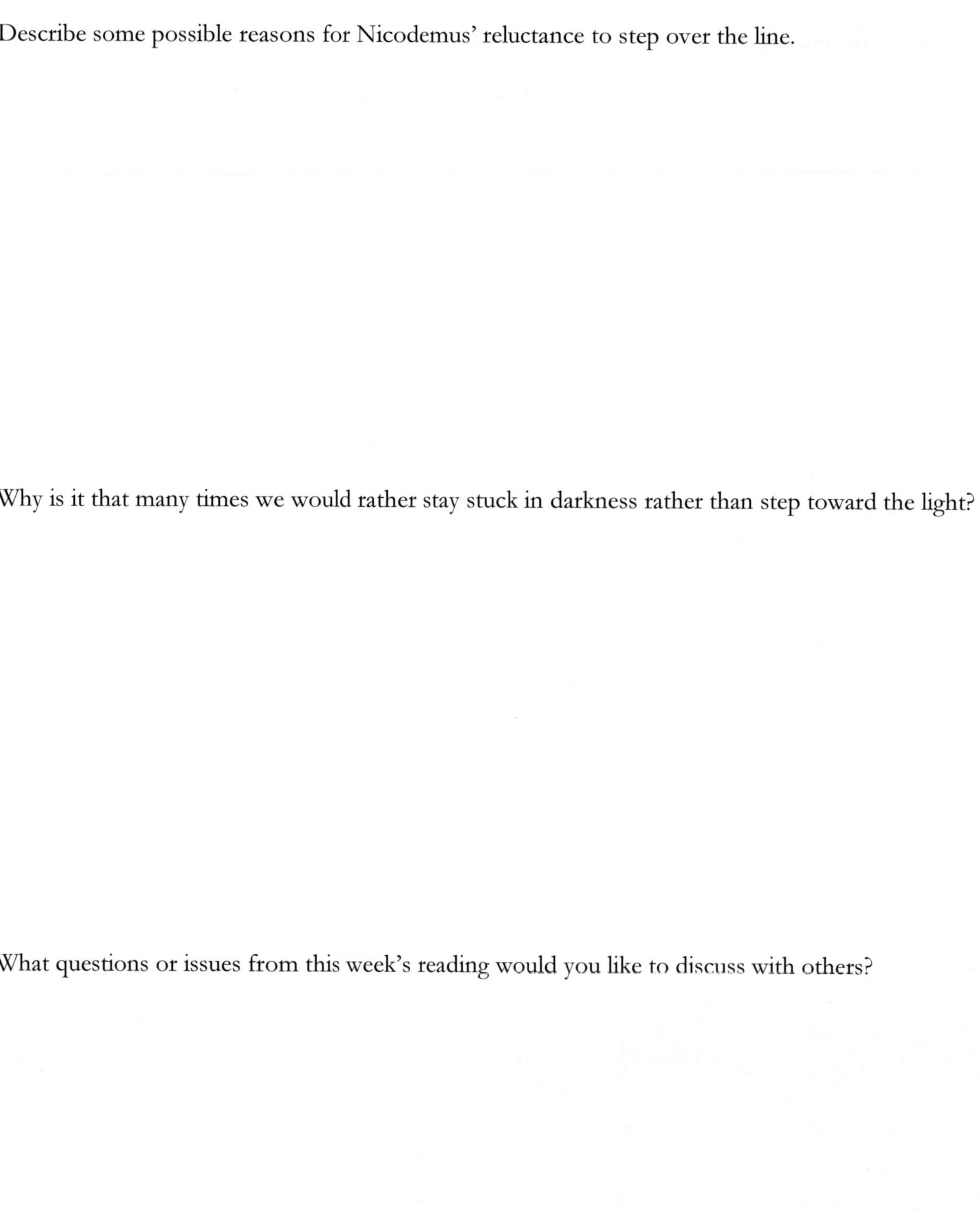

Describe some possible reasons for Nicodemus' reluctance to step over the line.

Why is it that many times we would rather stay stuck in darkness rather than step toward the light?

What questions or issues from this week's reading would you like to discuss with others?

Which of the Bible readings took on a new meaning for you this week?

How was your relationship to God deepened this week?

What one thing will you take away from this story of the encounter between Jesus and Nicodemus?

Chapter Five: Living Water

John 4:5-42 *So he came to a Samaritan city called Sychar, near the plot of ground that Jacob had given to his son Joseph. [6]Jacob's well was there, and Jesus, tired out by his journey, was sitting by the well. It was about noon. [7]A Samaritan woman came to draw water, and Jesus said to her, "Give me a drink." [8](His disciples had gone to the city to buy food.) [9]The Samaritan woman said to him, "How is it that you, a Jew, ask a drink of me, a woman of Samaria?" (Jews do not share things in common with Samaritans.) [10]Jesus answered her, "If you knew the gift of God, and who it is that is saying to you, 'Give me a drink,' you would have asked him, and he would have given you living water." [11]The woman said to him, "Sir, you have no bucket, and the well is deep. Where do you get that living water? [12]Are you greater than our ancestor Jacob, who gave us the well, and with his sons and his flocks drank from it?" [13]Jesus said to her, "Everyone who drinks of this water will be thirsty again, [14]but those who drink of the water that I will give them will never be thirsty. The water that I will give will become in them a spring of water gushing up to eternal life." [15]The woman said to him, "Sir, give me this water, so that I may never be thirsty or have to keep coming here to draw water." [16]Jesus said to her, "Go, call your husband, and come back." [17]The woman answered him, "I have no husband." Jesus said to her, "You are right in saying, 'I have no husband'; [18]for you have had five husbands, and the one you have now is not your husband. What you have said is true!" [19]The woman said to him, "Sir, I see that you are a prophet. [20]Our ancestors worshiped on this mountain, but you say that the place where people must worship is in Jerusalem." [21]Jesus said to her, "Woman, believe me, the hour is coming when you will worship the Father neither on this mountain nor in Jerusalem. [22]You worship what you do not know; we worship what we know, for salvation is from the Jews. [23]But the hour is coming, and is now here, when the true worshipers will worship the Father in spirit and truth, for the Father seeks such as these to worship him. [24]God is spirit, and those who worship him must worship in spirit and truth." [25]The woman said to him, "I know that Messiah is coming" (who is called Christ). "When he comes, he will proclaim all things to us." [26]Jesus said to her, "I am he, the one who is speaking to you." [27]Just then his disciples came. They were astonished that he was speaking with a woman, but no one said, "What do you want?" or, "Why are you speaking with her?" [28]Then the woman left her water jar and went back to the city. She said to the people, [29]"Come and see a man who told me everything I have ever done! He cannot be the Messiah, can he?" [30]They left the city and were on their way to him. [31]Meanwhile the disciples were urging him, "Rabbi, eat something." [32]But he said to them, "I have food to eat that you do not know about." [33]So the disciples said to one another, "Surely no one has brought him something to eat?" [34]Jesus said to them, "My food is to do the will of him who sent me and to complete his work. [35]Do you not say, 'Four months more, then comes the harvest'? But I tell you, look around you, and see how the fields are ripe for harvesting. [36]The reaper is already receiving wages and is gathering fruit for eternal life, so that sower and reaper may rejoice together. [37]For here the saying holds true, 'One sows and another reaps.' [38]I sent you to reap that for which you did not labor. Others have labored, and you have entered into their labor." [39]Many Samaritans from that city believed in him because of the woman's testimony, "He told me everything I have ever done." [40]So when the*

Samaritans came to him, they asked him to stay with them; and he stayed there two days. [41]And many more believed because of his word. [42]They said to the woman, "It is no longer because of what you said that we believe, for we have heard for ourselves, and we know that this is truly the Savior of the world."

Day 1: A Conversation at the Well

For the next several weeks, we will be reading about people who have "Life-Changing Encounters with Jesus." The conversation between Jesus and the Samaritan woman follows a similar pattern to the one between Jesus and Nicodemus (John 3:1-21). In both conversations Jesus takes the discussion to a deeper theological level. Because they are standing by a well, the Samaritan woman and Jesus begin by talking about water.

Nicodemus wonders what Jesus means by being born again or born from above. The woman at the well wonders how Jesus can give her a drink of Living Water without a bucket. They are very different people. Nicodemus is from the upper echelons of Jewish society. The woman is of ill repute. Nicodemus is a man of influence. She has a shady past. Nicodemus comes at night, seeking out Jesus. She comes to the well at the heat of the day hoping no one else would be there.

One thing that bothered, even scandalized, the religious leaders about Jesus was that he crossed social boundaries. For example, pious Jews would travel around the region of Samaria to avoid being defiled. Jesus had no such concerns about associating with "their kind." He travels right through the middle of Samaria. On the way he stops at a well for a rest and a drink. His disciples head into town for some take out. While Jesus is sitting on the well, a Samaritan woman approaches the well with her bucket.

Middle Eastern village women would avoid going to the well in the middle of the day; they would go early in the morning, and they would go in groups, for the sake of propriety. Jesus would be expected to withdraw from the well, avoiding eye contact, to allow her access without associating with her. But he breaks the social taboo, remains on the well, and even asks her for a drink.[40] Jesus shows a vulnerability; he's thirsty; he doesn't have a bucket; so he asks her for her help. Will she give him a drink?

She is astonished at his behavior. "Why are you even talking to me?" she asks him. After all, she's a Samaritan. She's a woman. And she's a woman alone.

Questions for reflection:

Why does Jesus take the time to speak to the Samaritan woman?

I do not know.

Are you more like Nicodemus or the Samaritan woman? Why?

Nicodemus I think...

Imagine meeting Jesus at your favorite watering hole. Just you and Jesus. And Jesus asks you, what are you really thirsting for most in your life? Go ahead and tell him.

This is hard for me to imagine and answer...

Prayer: *Father, empty me of all the "stuff" in my life. Help me be a vessel for your living water. Fill me to overflowing that I may spill your love on others. Thank you for your grace and overlooking my shortcomings. In Christ's name, Amen.*

Day 2: Knowing and Being Known

> ***John 4:5-9*** *So he came to a Samaritan city called Sychar, near the plot of ground that Jacob had given to his son Joseph. [6]Jacob's well was there, and Jesus, tired out by his journey, was sitting by the well. It was about noon. [7]A Samaritan woman came to draw water, and Jesus said to her, "Give me a drink." [8](His disciples had gone to the city to buy food.) [9]The Samaritan woman said to him, "How is it that you, a Jew, ask a drink of me, a woman of Samaria?" (Jews do not share things in common with Samaritans.)*

Their conversation was not supposed to happen. She was a woman. Jewish men did not talk publicly with women. She was a Samaritan and Jesus a Jew. Jews never talked to Samaritans. (Ever since their ancestors had returned from exile centuries before to their land with mixed blood and an impure religion, Jews considered Samaritans half-breed sinners.) Jesus was a rabbi and she was a woman, and beyond that, a woman of scandal–one might have realized this seeing her at the well in the midday heat. She was coming to the well alone in the middle of the day rather than in the morning or evening with the other women. The Samaritan woman expected Jesus to feel superior to her and to ignore her or even to insult her.

Jesus does the unexpected. He breaks the social conventions and trespasses the boundaries between them and asks her for a drink. And she expresses her shock: "How is it that you a Jew, ask a drink of me, a woman of Samaria?" (Jews wouldn't eat in the same room, let alone use the same vessel with a Samaritan.) Their conversation was not supposed to happen.

But they become involved in a conversation about thirst and water, and in John's gospel, such conversations are always on two levels. What she means by thirst is not quite the thirst that Jesus speaks about. She's thinking about water in the well; Jesus is thinking about a living water that quenches thirst forever.

Eventually they come to the real issue in her life, the painful place, perhaps the reason why she hauls water in the midday heat: the fact that she has had five husbands and is now living with a man who is not her husband. We do not know the circumstances of her life, what has led her to have 5 husbands. (Was she passed from brother to brother upon their deaths? Was she divorced several times? It was very easy for men to divorce their wives in that day). She tries to deflect the conversation away from herself and onto other subjects, like worship and religion.

The story of the woman at the well portrays the tension of human relationships. On the one hand we crave community. "As our lungs require air, so our souls require what only community provides. We were designed…to live in relationship."[41] It's why the employment promotion at Starbucks reads: "Create Community. Make a difference in someone's day...When you work at Starbucks, you can make a difference in someone's day by creating an environment where neighbors and friends can get together and reconnect while enjoying a great coffee experience."[42] We are people who crave relationship – why else would Starbucks promote coffee within that message about community?

But it's not that simple. We crave relationship, but we also fear intimacy, and therefore hide to prevent others from knowing us too deeply. (If he really knew me, if he saw me for who I really am, he would not like what he saw.) So we wear masks. And we erect walls. And we avoid intimacy. And we protect ourselves. "Some of us learn early in life to withhold ourselves from others, fearful of revealing who we truly are except to those we deeply trust…We learn such lessons from being hurt by another's knowledge of us. We fear that what others find out about us may cost us acceptance or love, so we avoid revealing our true selves."[43]

Questions for reflection:

Do you see this desiring-relationship-but-fearing-intimacy tension in your own life? How does it play out?

I fear vulnerability for in being vulnerable we open ourselves up to the possibility of pain – rejection, violence, threats, insults.

Yet Christ calls us to risk this does he not?

With whom are you free to be your true self? Who knows you really well? Give thanks to God for these people in your life. Or, if you cannot think of anyone, ask God for such a friend.

My wife. My child. A few close friends. Hunt Club.

Day 3: Real Community

"It is possible for people to attend the same church – even the same small group – sit in the same chair, nod to the same people, talk about sports, the weather, or even the Bible month after month, year after year, without anyone ever knowing them. Nobody knows their hopes, their fears. Nobody knows their marriage is crumbling, their heart is breaking. Nobody knows that they are involved in a secret pattern of sin that is destroying their soul."[44]

We want to be known yet we fear being known. How do we overcome these patterns of fear and hiding? In our gospel story, it happens as the woman grows in her knowledge of who Jesus is. At first, she sees him as a Jewish man. Then she recognizes that he is a prophet, a messenger of God. And finally, she hears Jesus identify himself to her as the Messiah. As she is known by Jesus the Messiah, her secrets need not be held inside any longer. Coming to know Jesus as Son of God, as Savior, and be known by him, can free us from our past.

> *"O LORD, you have searched me and known me. You know when I sit down and when I rise up; you discern my thoughts from far away. You search out my path and my lying down, and are acquainted with all my ways. Even before a word is on my tongue, O LORD, you know it completely." (Psalm 139:1-4)*

"We are known by God: wholly, deeply. God knows the best of us, the worst of us, the very parts we do not even understand about ourselves. And in Jesus Christ, we learn to know and trust that such knowledge aims not at our undoing but our renewing, not at our condemnation but our restoration."[45]

In the community of Christ, we are invited to remove our masks and live in the light, and acknowledge that we struggle with sin, and do stupid things, and want to live our own lives in our own ways. And we confess our sins and start again in the grace of God. Because of the good news of the gospel, because of Baptism and Holy Communion, and confession and forgiveness, the church has the opportunity to be a community of grace, a fellowship that experiences God's power to transform lives. The church can be a community that can lead people below the surface where "masks come off, conversations get deep, hearts get vulnerable, lives are shared, accountability is invited, and tenderness flows. People really do become like brothers and sisters. They shoulder each other's burdens."[46]

People all around us are looking for this experience of real community. They are looking for authentic relationships. They just don't expect to find them in a church. In the story, the woman invites the people of the village to come to meet the One who knows her completely. They meet Jesus and urge him to stay with them. He stays two days. And many come to believe. They see and experience for themselves that Jesus is the Christ, the Savior of the World (4:42).

At its best, the church is an authentic community that invites people to come to Jesus to be set free from their past and be given a future that is wide open. That they may meet the one in whom they will find Grace and Truth. And they will know for themselves that he is the one who will redefine the meaning of their lives. The Living Water who will quench every thirst.

Questions for reflection:

Who are the persons in your life that help to shoulder your burdens?

I don't know - perhaps this is one of the problems.

Have you experienced life in a community characterized by authentic relationships? If so, what was it like?

3BU is the closest I should think. This is why we miss each other so deeply and feel lonely so easily.

What spiritual resources exist within the Christian Church to encourage it to become such an authentic community?

For most, small groups hopefully introduce such meaningful friendships. But being a pastor of our church means we are different.

Prayer: *Thank you, Lord, for "the company of others on the journey, for those who demonstrate a keener vision of your commonwealth or a surer faith when all sight is lacking; for those who push on ahead to light the way or slow their steps to lend a hand in support of us; for those who help us to laugh at our own foolishness or hold us when we cry in our pain."*[47] *Amen.*

Day 4: Grace and Truth

The truth is that God knows us wholly. The grace is that God is merciful, slow to anger, and abounding in steadfast love. Knowing the grace and truth of God can free us from our past and give us a new life. For the woman at the well, Jesus knew the truth about her (he told her "everything" she ever did.) The grace is that Jesus establishes a relationship with her and offers her Living Water for her soul.

The truth is like a mirror held up to us, with the words, "This is your life and it's not pretty." The grace is that Christ came to save sinners and reconcile God's world to God. The truth: "If we say that we have no sin, we deceive ourselves, and the truth is not in us." The grace: "If we confess our sins, God who is faithful and just will forgive us our sins and cleanse us from all unrighteousness." (1 John 1:8-9)

Bonhoeffer writes: "In confession the break-through to new life occurs. Where sin is hated, admitted, and forgiven, there the break with the past is made."[48] Alcoholics Anonymous is based on the foundation of truth and grace, which leads to recovery. The truth: you cannot make it on your own. You are an alcoholic. The grace: There is a higher power, God, who can deliver you, and a community that will support you.

When Jesus offers the woman Living Water it is a metaphorical way of giving her the gift of eternal life, a place in God's kingdom, forgiveness, a new life. But she doesn't immediately jump at the offer. Perhaps she thinks there are strings attached.

For example, Jesus asks her to go get her husband. In doing so, he has brought up a subject about which she is likely ashamed. Jesus uncovers the truth that she has had a string of husbands and is now living with a man. She's not doing very well in the relationship department. We don't know why, but it seems to be the reason she comes to the well alone.

Evidently Jesus thinks it needs to be dealt with, acknowledged, confessed, if the woman is to experience real healing. But like many of us, she tries to avoid further personal exposure by changing the subject. Let's talk about something else…let's talk about religion. How about the different beliefs of the Jews and Samaritans? Which is the true religion, the Jews worshiping God in the temple in Jerusalem, or the Samaritans on Mount Gerizim in Samaria?

There are many ways we can avoid the truth. One way is to get stuck in the old arguments. If there are two sides, then I can make my argument and you can make yours and neither of us has to listen to the other. Who is right, or who can discredit the other, becomes more important than what is true, and the argument continues. And it's a safe, comfortable place to be, stuck in the old arguments.

Jesus doesn't play the old argument game. Jesus gets to the truth of her life, but not to condemn her. Jesus accepts her, cares for her, takes her seriously, challenges her, and offers her a new life a life that transcends the actions of her past.[49]

Questions for reflection:

Are you stuck in any old arguments? If so, which ones? (Pray to God to break you out of the rut.)

there always feels & seems like cycles as the same sins are always pressing in; as with the addict, my temptation and fall are regular & predictable

How has the grace and truth of God played out in your life? (Give thanks to God for the work of his Spirit in your life.)

The truth is I am unacceptable and unlovable, even now—
the grace is that I am accepted and I am loved.

If a mirror is held up to your life, what might be hard to acknowledge?

the lack of confrontation, lack of awareness
identity issues, joy issues

Does confession play any kind of regular role in your life? If so, what role?

yes and no; I confess but rarely
formally; thus I rarely receive formal forgiveness
but communion.

Day 5: A Life Changing Encounter

In her encounter with Jesus, the woman changes. She returns to the village without the water she had come for, or her bucket. But it seems she returns with living water that seems to be welling up inside her, like a spring that flows from her to others.

She goes from hiding from others and hiding from the truth to an honest acknowledgment of the truth, which is necessary for healing and wholeness to take place. She goes from avoiding people because she is embarrassed about something in her life, to boldly telling others about the one who just could be the Messiah. She goes from being stuck in her past to a freedom to live into the future. She becomes one of the first people to invite others to meet Jesus.

You don't have to have your life all together to point people to Jesus. You just have to know that he's the one who can give you a new life.

Jesus had a lengthy conversation with the woman at the well. Despite her history with men, her gender, and her Samaritan roots, Jesus took her seriously and taught her about living water and eternal life. Jesus gave her hope.[50] Life did not have to be limited by her past, but could be shaped anew, or should we say afresh, by the grace of God, like a drink of cool fresh water, for a parched, thirsty person.

Questions for reflection:

How can a simple conversation at the well (or at the bar) become a life-changing blessing to someone?

Have you ever participated in conversations that began with simple topics like the weather, or work, and moved into deeper discussions about faith and God?

Did you have an opportunity recently to offer someone a word of hope, or did someone recently offer you a word of hope? What happened?

Prayer: *"Merciful God, the fountain of living water, your quench our thirst and wash away our sin. Give us this water always. Bring us to drink from the well that flows with the beauty of your truth through Jesus Christ, Our Savior and Lord."*[51] *Amen.*

Day 6: A Word to Share (Russ Melton)

Why do we keep doing the same things and expecting different results? I've heard that this is the definition of insanity. It seems like we are afraid to follow Christ. It is easier to continue to do what we know is wrong.

No matter what we have done in the past, Christ offers us a "do over." Not only that, He can take an ordinary person (or someone with a questionable reputation) and use them to reach others.

I'm part of a group that visits men in the local jail to share God's love. I hope that it helps the men that are incarcerated, but I KNOW it blesses me! These men have powerful stories. Even though they have made mistakes, God uses them to witness to the other men in jail and also those of us who visit. God has a mission for them right where they are. Even though most of these men are "different" from me, we are brothers in Christ. They can experience the same "living water" that I have. God offers us all the same grace through His son, Jesus. None of us deserves it, but he gives it to us anyway.

I would challenge you to step out of your comfort zone. Jesus went to an area that Jews considered inhabited by spiritual and ethnic half-breeds. He stopped to talk to a woman who was very different from him ethnically and morally. What might be God calling you to do? Don't miss the opportunity to do God's work. It could be as simple as stopping by someone's house to see how they are doing or stopping by a co-workers desk that you've been avoiding. We are *all* called to do God's work (not just pastors). Just like the inmates are uniquely qualified to witness to others in their cell block, you are uniquely qualified to witness to the people in your life. The woman at the well was so excited about meeting Jesus that she went back to her community and shared the good news. Let's forget about our own fears and start living for Christ.

Questions for reflection:

Do you know of people who would feel rejected by the "Christian Church," but whom Jesus could embrace through you?

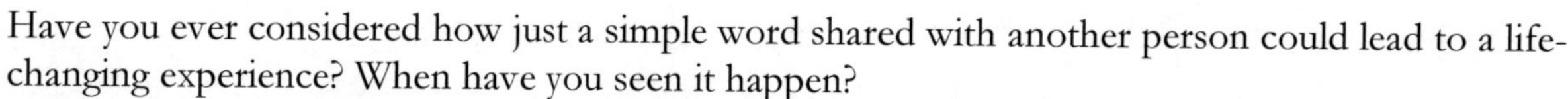

Have you ever considered how just a simple word shared with another person could lead to a life-changing experience? When have you seen it happen?

Prayer: *Thank you, God, for handcrafting us in a way that we can bless those around us. Help us to recognize Christ in our lives. Help us recognize opportunities to witness to others about your love. Thank you for your grace. Amen.*

Taking It Further: Small Group and Chapter Summary Questions

If you are participating in a small group with this study, how is the group progressing toward authentic community? Are you staying more on a "safe" level, or are you risking going below the surface?

In the encounter with the Samaritan woman at the well (John 4:1-26), Jesus offers her "living water" that will quench her thirst forever. What do you think she was looking for in her life? What do you think she really needed?

What kind of spiritual refreshment is Jesus offering the Samaritan woman?

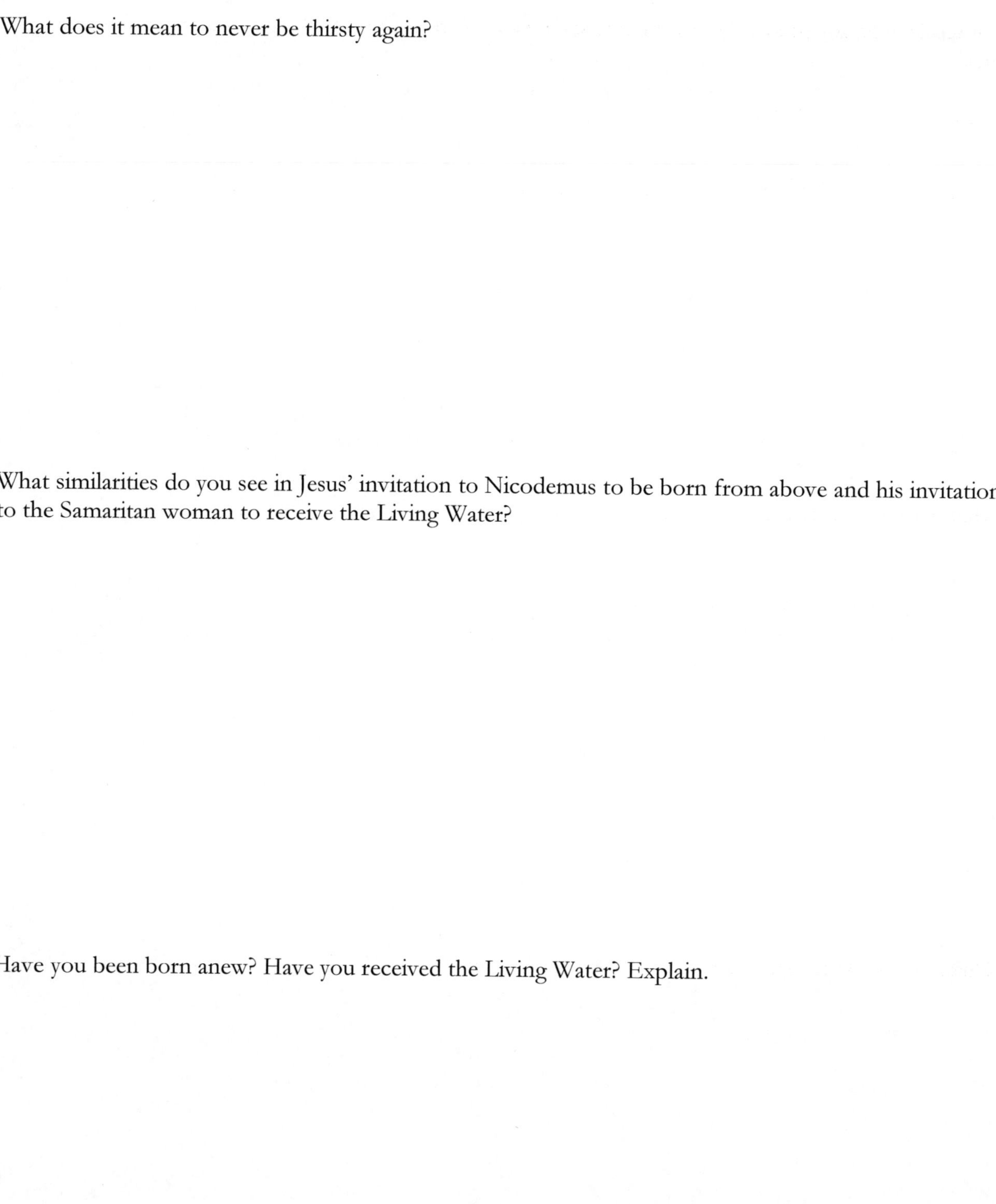

What does it mean to never be thirsty again?

What similarities do you see in Jesus' invitation to Nicodemus to be born from above and his invitation to the Samaritan woman to receive the Living Water?

Have you been born anew? Have you received the Living Water? Explain.

Is it challenging for you to share your true self or your faith with others? If so, what is holding you back?

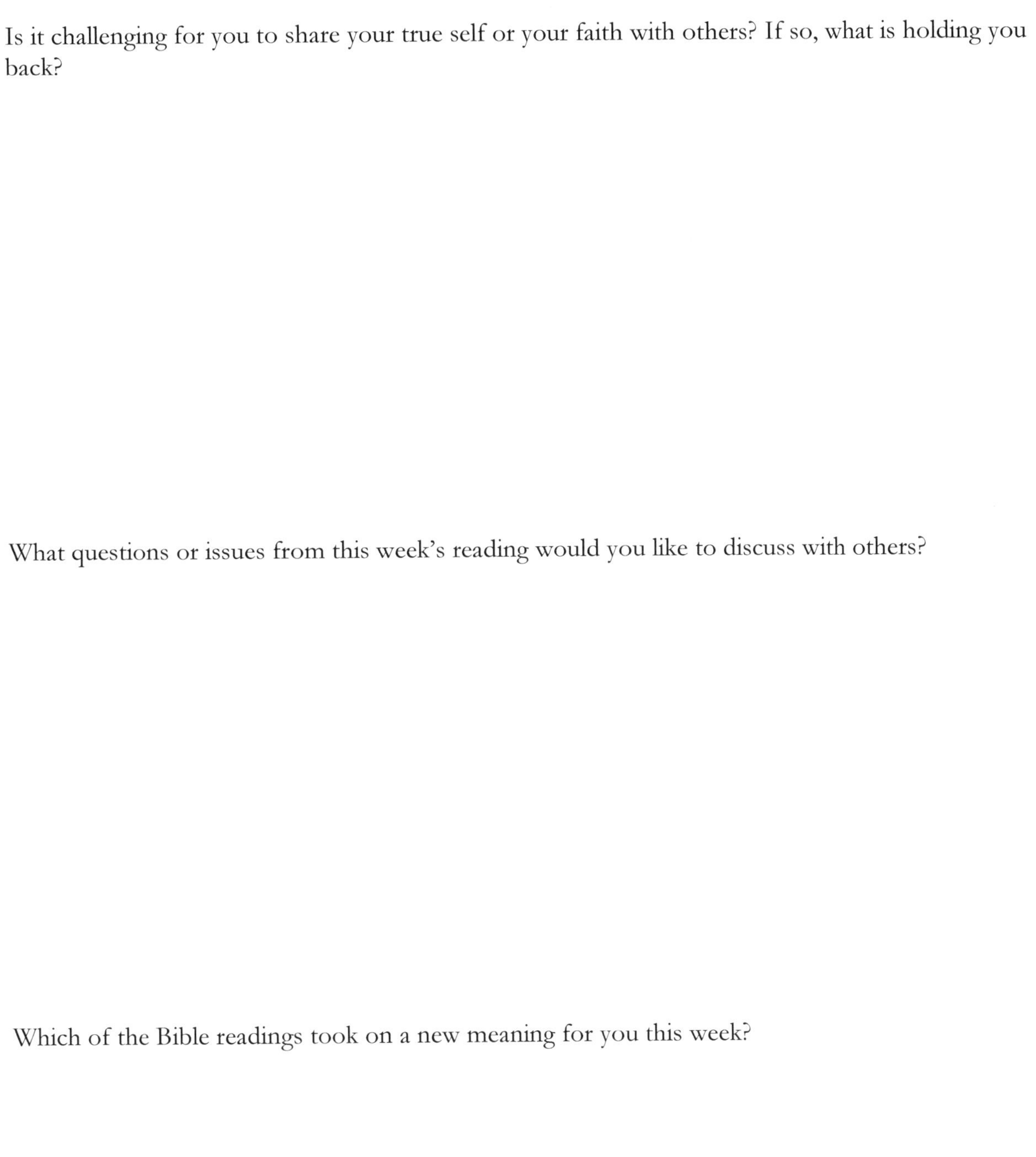

What questions or issues from this week's reading would you like to discuss with others?

Which of the Bible readings took on a new meaning for you this week?

How was your relationship to God deepened this week?

What one thing do you take away from this story of the encounter between Jesus and the Samaritan woman?

Recommended resources for further study:

Kenneth Bailey, *Jesus Through Middle Eastern Eyes: Cultural Studies in the Gospels*

Dietrich Bonhoeffer, *Life Together*

Andy Stanley and Bill Willets, *Creating Community: Five Keys to Building a Small Group Culture*

Chapter Six: Was Blind but Now I See

Jesus Heals a Blind Man (John 9:1-41)

Scene 1 – (John 9:1-7) opens with Jesus and his disciples walking by and observing a blind man. He is likely begging with many others outside the temple gates. The disciples ask a theological question (who sinned?). Jesus gives sight to the blind man.[52]

Scene 2 – (8-12) takes place in the blind man's neighborhood. Friends and neighbors are discussing: is this man who can see the same man as the one born blind? They ask him many questions. He tells them what he knows.

Scene 3 – (13-17) The man is hauled before the religious authorities. This has become a religious matter, being a miracle, and being done on the Sabbath. The authorities are divided: an act of God, say some; a criminal breach of the law, say others. They turn to the man himself – what does he think? He says Jesus is a prophet. They reject his witness and look for more evidence.

Scene 4 – (18-23) The man's parents stand fearful before the authorities. It has become clear that not only is Jesus on trial, but also anyone who believes in him. They distance themselves from Jesus and from their son. They don't want to be involved.

Scene 5 – (24-34) The man is brought back before the authorities for more aggressive questioning. They want the man to go along with their plan to denounce Jesus as a lawbreaker and sinner. And it begins to look as if the man himself is on trial for being a follower of Jesus. "The man's faith and courage have now grown stronger even though he stands alone without the support of neighbors or parents."[53] They expel him from the synagogue.

Scene 6 – (35-41) Jesus finds the man and reveals himself to him. The man now confesses his faith in Jesus and worships him.

Day 1: The Light of the World (Paul St. Clair)

> ***John 9:6-12*** *When he had said this, he spat on the ground and made mud with the saliva and spread the mud on the man's eyes, [7]saying to him, "Go, wash in the pool of Siloam" (which means Sent). Then he went and washed and came back able to see. [8]The neighbors and those who had seen him before as a beggar began to ask, "Is this not the man who used to sit and beg?" [9]Some were saying, "It is he." Others were saying, "No, but it is someone like him." He kept saying, "I am the man." [10]But they kept asking him, "Then how were your eyes opened?" [11]He answered, "The man called Jesus made mud, spread it on my eyes, and said to me, 'Go to Siloam and wash.' Then I went and washed and received my sight." [12]They said to him, "Where is he?" He said, "I do not know."*

Someone suggested how the church ended up with so many denominations. Their theory goes back to the different ways Jesus chose to heal people who were blind. On one occasion he simply spoke and the man was healed. On another he touched the man and he was healed. On another he spit on some dirt, made mud and put it on the man's eyes. He healed all three, but in different ways. Supposedly denominations began when the three formerly blind men argued over the correct way to be healed. You have the Muddites, the Touchites and the Word Alone folks. Each group insists their way is right.

Why did Jesus heal the man in this way, instead of in his usual way (instantaneous upon speaking the word)? The best explanation is that he was again addressing the controversy with the Pharisee's concerning their Sabbath laws. Jesus healed the man on a Sabbath. Rabbinic teaching had perverted this humane Old Testament provision into a straight-jacket catalogue of Blue Laws. In healing this man on the Sabbath, Jesus violated four of their rules: plowing (spittle rolling on the dirt), kneading (making the clay), anointing (putting clay on the man's eyes), and of course healing (illegal unless a life-threatening emergency). Jesus hated the way man-made religion elevated ritual observance over human need, and never hesitated to break its rules. Once again, his actions precipitate a conflict over his identity. But there is more going on here than a spectacular healing miracle or a protest against unbiblical Blue Laws.

John is careful to tell us that Jesus performs this miracle "having said these words." What words? The words in John 8:12, "While I am in the world, I am the light of the world." Like all of the miracles in John, this one was also a "sign" (an "attesting miracle," revealing Jesus' ability to meet humanity's spiritual needs.) The miracle validates Jesus' claim to be the Light of the World. At the Feast of Tabernacles huge lamps were lit in the Temple to commemorate the pillar of fire in the wilderness – signifying God's presence and guidance. Jesus is now claiming to be God's source of spiritual enlightenment to a spiritually blind humanity.

Questions for reflection:

A blind man is healed by the Light of the World. What symbolism do you see in this encounter?

What does it mean to you that Jesus is the Light of the World and the light of your life?

Prayer: *O Light of the World, shine the light of your presence in my life today. Lead me, reassure me, and cleanse me by your light. Amen.*

Day 2: Eyes Opened (Paul St. Clair)

> ***John 9:10-11*** *"'How then were your eyes opened?' they demanded. [11]He replied, 'The man they call Jesus made some mud and put it on my eyes. He told me to go to Siloam and wash. So I went and washed, and then I could see.'"*

I love cartoons. One of my favorites is about two Eskimos fishing through the ice.

In the first scene the Eskimo is fishing through a hole he has cut in the ice which is the size of a grapefruit. The second scene is about a second Eskimo cutting his own hole in the ice. This hole is huge. It is literally big enough to drag a whale through. Sometimes we drill our holes too small.

We are like the little girl who was asked by her Sunday School teacher to participate in a letter writing ministry for one of the missionaries. The teacher explained that the missionary lived far away and was very busy, so she may not be able to reply to their letter for some time. The little girl wrote, "Dear Missionary Carter. I am praying for you. I really don't expect an answer." "We do not receive," James (4:2) says, "because we do not ask". Through the prophet God told the people to "Call upon me and I will show you great and mighty things which you do not know I can do"

Where there is no vision the people perish. Think of what a compelling vision can mean, how it can shape individuals, even whole peoples. With a vision of his own divine destiny, Alexander the Great, in a 13 year rule, led little Macedonia to unprecedented conquests and world empire. When John Kennedy was given a vision of a space program, he said, "Let's go for it," and the whole country was committed to putting a person on the moon.

The blind man's eyes were not the only ones opened that day. The disciples were beginning to realize this man Jesus was more than a carpenter, more than an itinerant preacher. He was doing things that no mortal could do. The prophet Isaiah said when the Messiah came "the Spirit of the Lord would be upon him to preach the good news to the poor…bind up the brokenhearted, proclaim freedom to the captives and release those imprisoned by darkness." (Isaiah 61:1) The disciples are witnessing these events in their midst.

Questions for reflection:

Like the blind man, we are sent to wash (baptism), and we encounter the light of the world, and we come to see in a new way. In what ways have your eyes been opened? Offer a prayer of thanksgiving to God for this work in your life.

What examples do you see today of Christ's ongoing mission: good news to the poor, binding up the brokenhearted, freedom to captives, and release of those imprisoned by darkness?

Day 3: Revised Beliefs

> ***Acts 10:34-43*** *Then Peter began to speak to them: "I truly understand that God shows no partiality, [35]but in every nation anyone who fears him and does what is right is acceptable to him. [36]You know the message he sent to the people of Israel, preaching peace by Jesus Christ – he is Lord of all. [37]That message spread throughout Judea, beginning in Galilee after the baptism that John announced: [38]how God anointed Jesus of Nazareth with the Holy Spirit and with power; how he went about doing good and healing all who were oppressed by the devil, for God was with him. [39]We are witnesses to all that he did both in Judea and in Jerusalem. They put him to death by hanging him on a tree; [40]but God raised him on the third day and allowed him to appear, [41]not to all the people but to us who were chosen by God as witnesses, and who ate and drank with him after he rose from the dead. [42]He commanded us to preach to the people and to testify that he is the one ordained by God as judge of the living and the dead. [43]All the prophets testify about him that everyone who believes in him receives forgiveness of sins through his name."*

Pastor Richard Lischer tells this story. "In a church I served, one of the pillars of the congregation stopped by my office just before services to tell me he'd been 'born again.'

'You've been what?' I asked.

'I visited my brother-in-law's church, the Running River of Life Tabernacle, and I don't know what it was, but something happened and I'm born again.'

'You can't be born again,' I said, 'you're a Lutheran. You are the chairman of the board of trustees.'

He was brimming with joy, but I was sulking. Why? Because spiritual renewal is wonderful as long as it occurs within acceptable, usually mainline, channels and does not threaten my understanding of God."[54]

Pastor Lischer found himself in a similar place as the Pharisees, where he had to deal with a spiritual event that fell outside of his own expectations and accepted tradition.

The Pharisees interview a man who was born blind, who can now see. They ask how his eyes were opened. "As they try to impose their preconceived beliefs on this experience they start to deny the experience rather than question their beliefs. 'Since the cure is on the Sabbath this man can't be from God.' 'Perhaps the man was never blind to begin with.' 'The blind man can't teach us anything since he has obviously been a sinner since birth.'[55]

Sometimes growing in faith means moving from old inadequate beliefs to new beliefs based on new insights given by God through God's Word and certain experiences.

Remember (in Acts 10) how Peter had to grow out of his old beliefs when he had a vision in which he heard God telling him to eat an assortment of animals that Peter had been previously taught were unclean. It was a new revelation that led Peter to take the message about Jesus Christ to the gentiles, (the non-Jews), starting with Cornelius and his household at Caesarea. This began an entirely new mission focus for the young Christian Church.

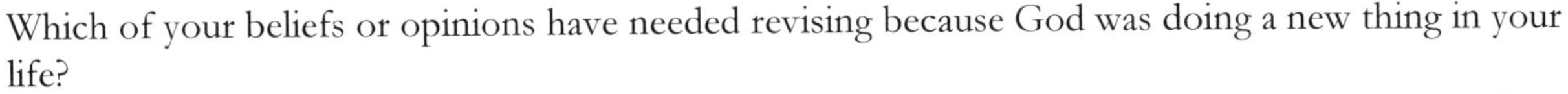

Questions for reflection:

Which of your beliefs or opinions have needed revising because God was doing a new thing in your life?

How did Peter discern that it was God who was giving him a new revelation? (Acts 10)

Prayer: *Where do my beliefs need revising, Lord? What views am I holding on to that prevent your truth from its work? Amen.*

Day 4: A Faith Story

Sometimes in a mission team preparation meeting, Nancy Schmitz has told the participants that at the next meeting, the participants will begin to share their testimonies. And people have asked, share my what?

Typically Baptists are good at that, but Lutherans not so much. But we're getting more comfortable with sharing parts of our faith stories, aren't we? We're getting more comfortable being in the Word together, and praying together, and talking about God and faith and life, not only with each other, but with people outside the church walls. One of the primary reasons we've improved in those disciplines is because of the impact of discipleship groups and small group participation.

In the case of the blind man whom Jesus healed, we can see his progressive steps of faith in Jesus. It all begins when he meets Jesus, who applies dirt and spit to his eyes, and instructs him to go and wash. Upon doing this, he receives his sight. He quickly believes that Jesus is a miracle worker (Jesus opened his eyes). As he is interviewed by the religious authorities, the man professes that Jesus must be a prophet. Then he recognizes Jesus must be from God. Finally, he worships Jesus.

The man did not really have his faith story all figured out. He did not know all the correct religious phrases. He didn't understand much of who Jesus was. He was not pious or even respectful of his elders. But he knows what he knows. "One thing I know…that though I was blind, now I see." (9:25) "What he knew for sure was that once upon a time he sat in darkness, and now the whole world was drenched in sunlight."[56]

Questions for reflection:

What would the man want to mention if he were asked to tell his faith story?

The man came to a progressively deeper awareness of who Jesus was. In what ways have you come to a deeper awareness of who Jesus is?

Often it is when we look back upon the events of our lives that we see God's hand guiding us. Share an example from your own life.

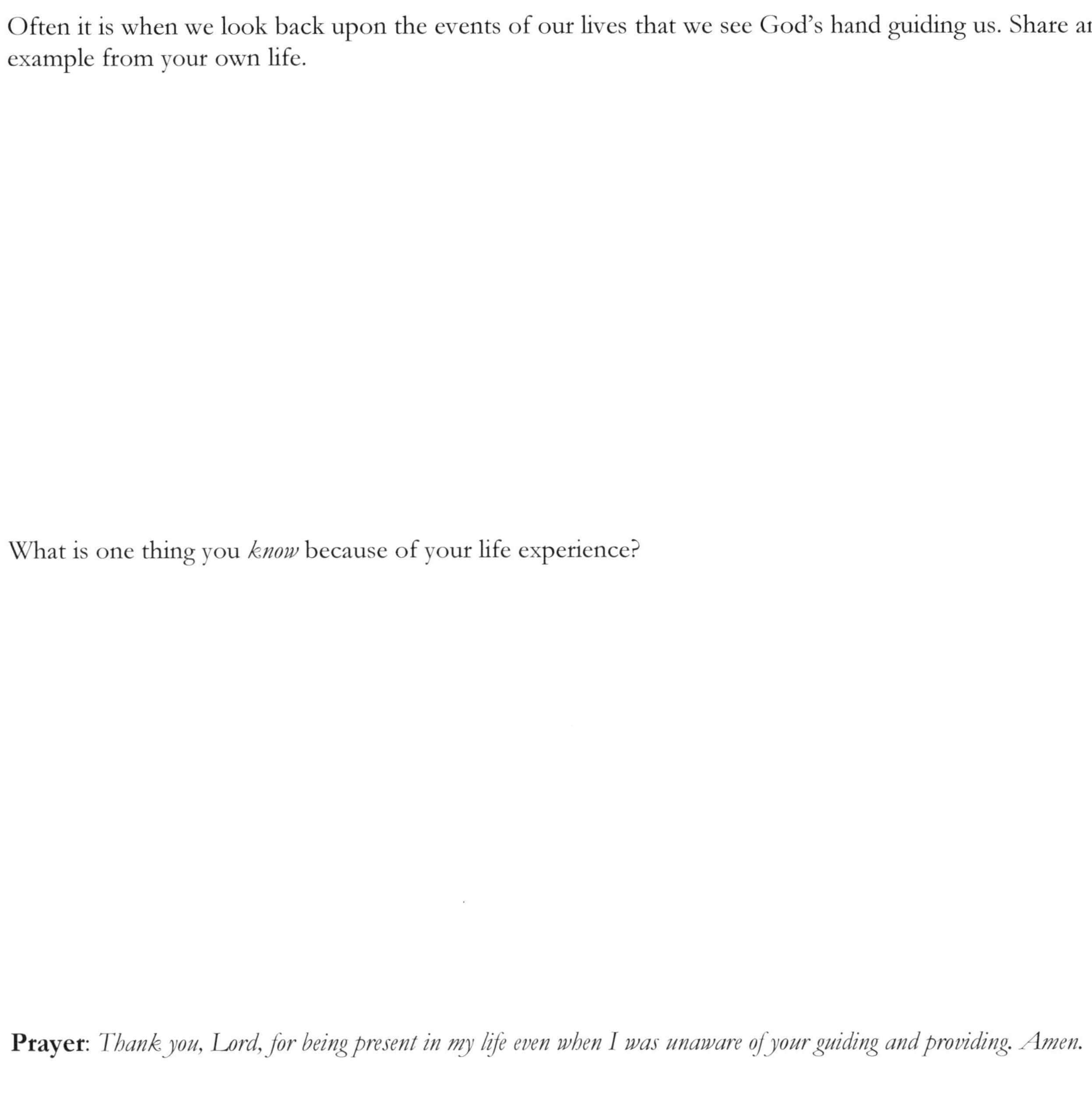

What is one thing you *know* because of your life experience?

Prayer: *Thank you, Lord, for being present in my life even when I was unaware of your guiding and providing. Amen.*

Day 5: Against the Grain

In this brief encounter with Jesus, the formerly blind man quickly discovers that not everyone is happy about his healing. Following Jesus is not a case where one believes in Jesus and all one's problems go away. His healing and his new-found faith seem to bring about more problems.

Sometimes your faith sets you at odds with the world around you, even with your family and friends. There are many places in the world where becoming a Christian forces you to leave your family and your town. In some places you risk death by confessing Jesus Christ as Lord.

This man had been so little trouble as a blind beggar. But because of his healing, he now poses a real problem for the religious authorities. And finally he is kicked out of the synagogue. Sometimes there's a cost to having your eyes opened. You may feel like a stranger in a strange land – not fitting in or as welcome as you were before.

Ask one of the people who returns from a mission trip. One woman describes it like this: Your eyes get opened about something, and the haunting begins. You start to notice how much of your life is based on materialism. Or you look at all your things and you ask yourself, how did I get here?

It can also happen when you decide to stand with the oppressed and the poor in your community, and you begin to recognize that you are questioning the status quo. It's something like swimming upstream, or going against the grain.

Questions for reflection:

Have you had to rethink some of your long held beliefs because of some life event or new insight? Explain.

What was your most recent eye opening experience?

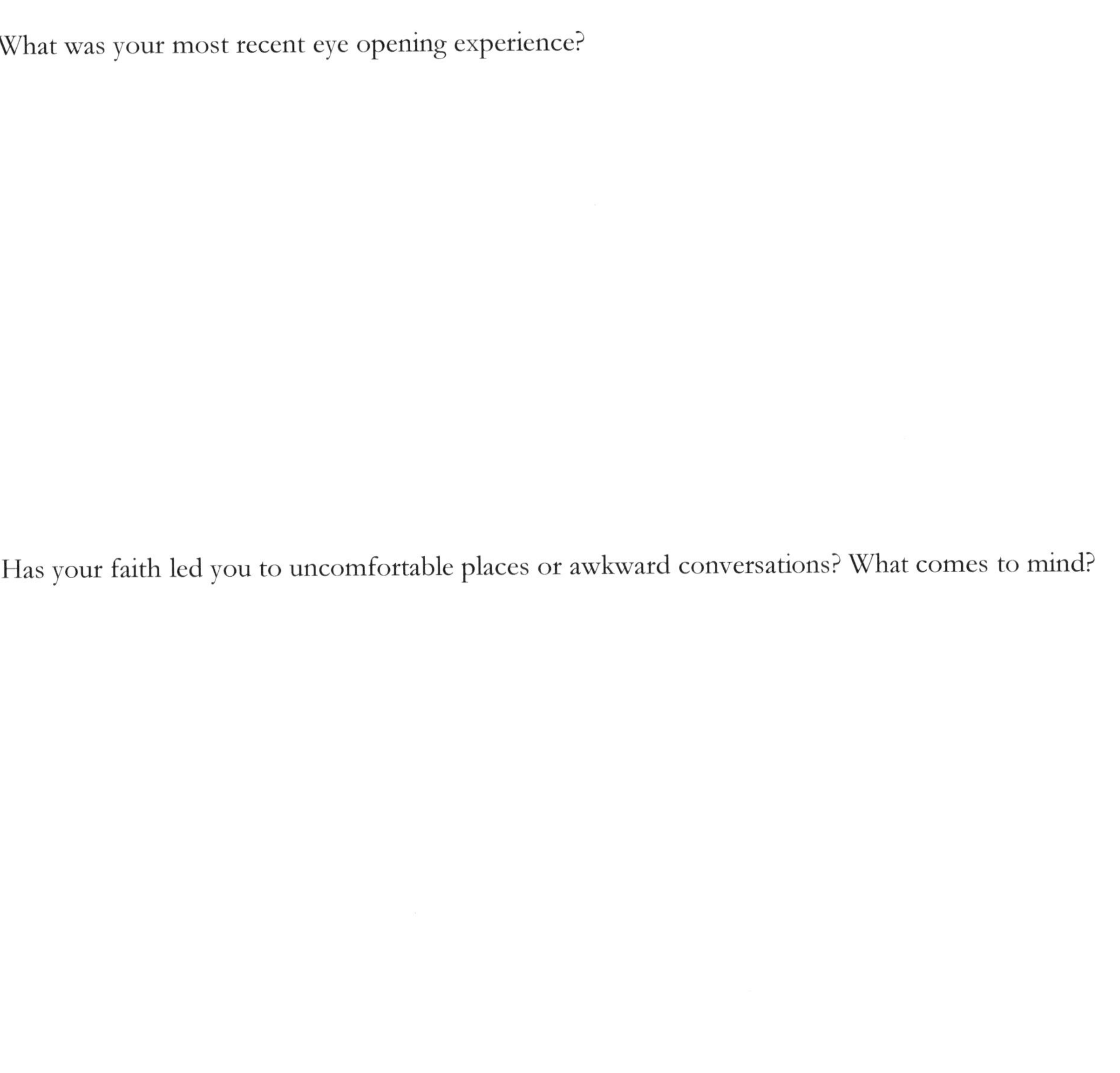

Has your faith led you to uncomfortable places or awkward conversations? What comes to mind?

Day 6: Questions

The healed man reverses the investigation and asks the Pharisees, "Do you also want to become his disciples?" (John 9:27) Later, he adds, "If this man were not from God, he could do nothing." (John 9:33) The reaction by the Pharisees is strong. They are insulted by his comments, and drive him out. As the "blind man" comes to see the light of Christ, the Pharisees reveal their own blindness.

Jesus responds by seeking him for conversation and consolation. At their second meeting, the healed man takes the opportunity to confess his faith in Jesus, reflecting his own physical *and* spiritual transformation. The healed man is a grateful seeker who wants a better understanding about the One who healed him. At this point, it does not matter what others say. The healed man is looking face to face at his savior, the One who healed him, the One from God. With that he confesses his belief and begins to worship Jesus. "I once was lost but now am found, was blind but now I see."

The story leaves us with some challenging questions. Spend some time with the questions that catch your attention.

Who are the real "sinners" in the story?

Who really is blind, and who can see?

What does it mean to be spiritually blind? Blind to the revelation of God?

Where do you find yourself in the story? With whom do you identify?

What were the blind spots for the Pharisees?

Do you know any of your own blind spots? What are they?

How do you become aware of your spiritual blind spots?

Prayer: *Where am I blind to what you want to reveal to me, Lord? In what ways do I have a hard heart or a closed mind? Amen.*

Taking It Further: Small Group and Chapter Summary Questions

Probably the most well known hymn within the Christian Church is John Newton's *Amazing Grace*.

Amazing grace! how sweet the sound
that saved a wretch like me!
I once was lost, but now am found;
was blind, but now I see.

'Twas grace that taught my heart to fear,
and grace my fears relieved;
how precious did that grace appear
the hour I first believed!

Through many dangers, toils, and snares
I have already come;
'tis grace has brought me safe thus far,
and grace will lead me home.

The Lord has promised good to me;
his word my hope secures;
he will my shield and portion be
as long as life endures.

When we've been there ten thousand years,
bright shining as the sun,
we've no less days to sing God's praise
than when we'd first begun.

(John Newton, 1725-1807, alt., stzs 1-4; anonymous, st. 5.)

John Newton meditates on the amazing grace of God. What do you think is most amazing about God's grace?

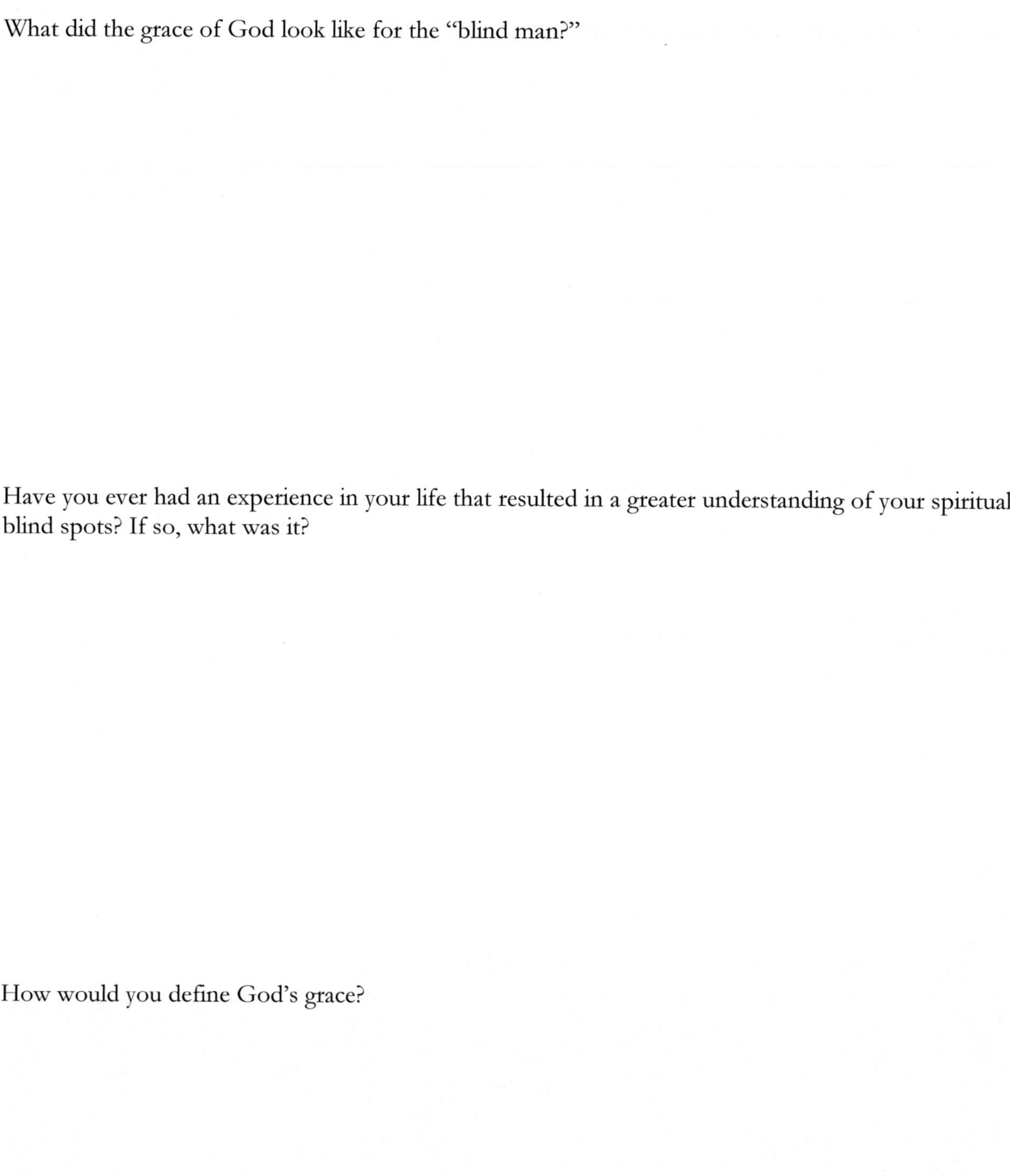

What did the grace of God look like for the "blind man?"

Have you ever had an experience in your life that resulted in a greater understanding of your spiritual blind spots? If so, what was it?

How would you define God's grace?

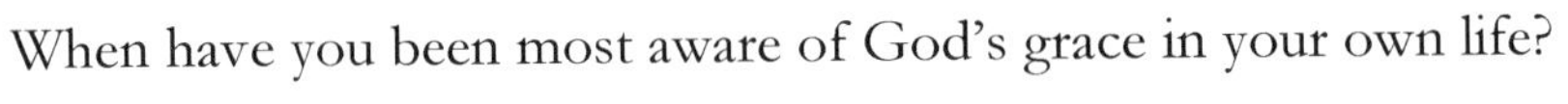

When have you been most aware of God's grace in your own life?

What questions or issues from this week's reading would you like to discuss with others?

How was your relationship to God deepened this week?

What one thing do you take away from this story of the healing of the blind man?

Chapter Seven: Forgiven

John 8:2-11 *Early in the morning he came again to the temple. All the people came to him and he sat down and began to teach them. [3]The scribes and the Pharisees brought a woman who had been caught in adultery; and making her stand before all of them, [4]they said to him, "Teacher, this woman was caught in the very act of committing adultery. [5]Now in the law Moses commanded us to stone such women. Now what do you say?" [6]They said this to test him, so that they might have some charge to bring against him. Jesus bent down and wrote with his finger on the ground. [7]When they kept on questioning him, he straightened up and said to them, "Let anyone among you who is without sin be the first to throw a stone at her." [8]And once again he bent down and wrote on the ground. [9]When they heard it, they went away, one by one, beginning with the elders; and Jesus was left alone with the woman standing before him. [10]Jesus straightened up and said to her, "Woman, where are they? Has no one condemned you?" [11]She said, "No one, sir." And Jesus said, "Neither do I condemn you. Go your way, and from now on do not sin again."*

Day 1: A Scandal

The story is not found in some of the early manuscripts, perhaps because it is so scandalous. One scandal is that the story is about a woman caught in adultery. But the real scandal is that Jesus lets her off without punishment. Just how far is grace supposed to go?

On the last day of the Festival of Booths (John 7), when water was brought from the Pool of Siloam in a procession to the Temple, Jesus does something rather controversial. As the water is being carried to the temple, Jesus calls out: "Let anyone who is thirsty come to me, and let the one who believes in me drink. As the scripture has said, 'Out of the believer's heart shall flow rivers of living water.'" (The Gospel of John tells us that Jesus was referring to the Holy Spirit.)

When some people hear Jesus they feel that he must be a prophet or the Messiah. Others scoff at the idea – neither a prophet nor the Messiah would come from Galilee. And there is disagreement among the chief priests, Pharisees and temple police about who Jesus is and if he should be arrested.

The very next morning we see that the Pharisees have quickly devised a plan to trap Jesus. They want to get Jesus to say something that will get him into trouble, so they will have the necessary evidence against him, to arrest him. As Jesus is teaching, suddenly he is interrupted by a group of men who have with them a woman they had caught in the act of adultery. (Now how between the night and the next morning did they find this woman? Evidently she also was trapped. She is found in bed with a man who wasn't her husband. Since it takes two to commit adultery, where is the man?)

"Teacher," they say, "The Law of Moses says this woman deserves to be stoned to death. What do you say?" The law stipulates that if a man commits adultery with the wife of his neighbor, both the adulterer and the adulteress shall be put to death (Lev 20:10). It was seldom enforced. Under Roman rule it was illegal for Jewish courts to enforce a death sentence. But that did not always succeed in preventing stoning (Acts 7:58-59).[57]

They were using the woman to get at Jesus. It was controversial. It would draw a crowd. It would put Jesus on the spot. They wanted to publicly humiliate Jesus. They are trying to trap Jesus to discredit him in the eyes of the authorities in Jerusalem. They quote the law of Moses and challenge Jesus to agree or disagree. They assumed there were only two options. If he agreed with the Law of Moses, they would force his hand; the mob could stone her, and the Romans would descend upon them to stamp out the commotion. And Jesus would be arrested.

But they didn't think he would choose that option. They had heard his talk about grace and seen him associate with other sinners and law-breakers. They knew that Jesus seemed to always be on the side of the outcasts, tax collectors and sinners. They suspect that he might go against the Law of Moses and turn this woman loose. Then they would have him. He would be branded a heretic; he would be discredited. It's a lose-lose situation.

But rather than choose either option, "Jesus places himself between the leaders and the woman."[58] Jesus intercedes.

Question for reflection:

What do you think….how far should grace go? Do you have a concern that grace accepts or condones the sin as well as the sinner?

Prayer: *"O Lord God, merciful judge, you are the inexhaustible fountain of forgiveness. Replace our hearts of stone with hearts that love and adore you, that we may delight in doing your will, through Jesus Christ, our Savior and Lord. Amen."*[59]

Day 2: Calling the Question

They stand there with stones in their hands, waiting for his word. Jesus does a curious thing. Jesus appears disinterested in the scandal. He bends down and starts writing in the sand. Then he says, "Go ahead and throw your stones if you want. Just make sure you are sinless yourself."

Why did Jesus write in the sand? The eighth day of the feast was treated as a Sabbath, with all the Sabbath laws in force. Writing – making a permanent mark – was forbidden. But writing with one's finger in the dust was permissible because it leaves no permanent mark.[60]

What did Jesus write in the sand? And why did he write it instead of just speaking it? We don't know what he wrote, but I like Ray Stedman's interpretation.[61] Perhaps Jesus wrote the four words that were written once before by the finger of God. The Pharisees and religious leaders, when seeing the four words, would immediately know their meaning. They come from the book of Daniel, where King Belshazzar held a great feast that turned into drunkenness and debauchery. When he ate and drank from the sacred vessels from the temple in Jerusalem, he blasphemed God. In the midst of their revelry, a great hand appeared and wrote four words on the wall, "Mene, Mene, Tekel, Upharsin." The prophet Daniel was called in to interpret them, and he gave them this interpretation: "You are weighed in the balance and found wanting." (Daniel 5:25-29)

Maybe that's why Jesus wrote it instead of speaking it. The hand of God that judged King Belshazzar now writes the same words again, but this time they are addressed to self-righteous conspirators who are using a woman to trap Jesus. ("You are weighed in the balance and found wanting.") And Jesus adds, "Let anyone among you who is without sin be the first to throw a stone at her." (John 8:7)

Questions for reflection:

What are your ideas about what Jesus might have written in the sand?

What do you think…are some sins worse than other sins? Does Jesus equalize degrees of sin by inviting those who have no sin to throw the first stone at the woman?

Day 3: A Second Chance

Jesus puts the choice back in their hands. Since the law says she deserves to be stoned, go ahead…but let the one who is without sin throw the first stone.

The law stipulates that the witnesses throw the first stones. (Jesus adds one thing to the requirement. They need to be innocent. Is there anyone here who has never sinned?

The person without sin can throw the first stone.)[62]

Have you noticed that pointing out the sins of others helps to deflect attention away from our own sins? But scripture (1 John 1:8) reminds us: "if we claim to be without sin, we deceive ourselves and the truth is not in us."

The woman is accused, but not condemned. She receives no punishment. Jesus sets her free to live a new life. "The past – hers and ours – isn't the point. The Lord is more interested in our future."[63]

One by one, stones are dropped from tightly clenched fists, and the accusers leave. (Thinking they would humiliate Jesus, they are now put to shame.)

"Where are they?" Jesus asks her. "Is there no one left to condemn you?"

"No one sir."

(When the witnesses and accusers leave, the case falls apart. The jury has been dismissed.) "I do not condemn you either. Go, but do not sin again."

Jesus has the right to condemn her. (He is the only sinless one who could throw a stone at her.) But Jesus treats her as a person, not an outcast. He treats her with respect…with truth and grace. He gives her another chance.

Does Jesus belittle the sin? No, he challenges her to leave it. She is forgiven, and she is also given a command to go and sin no more. Jesus forgives her to set her free to live a different life. You do not need to be bound by your sin. Choose a new road. Live a new life. (God loves us and accepts us as we are, but his love does not want us to remain where we are.)

Imagine yourself standing accused. Maybe you were not caught in adultery, but there is some other sin. A sinfulness that you cannot overcome. There you stand, having continually disobeyed God. Having hurt others as well as yourself.

You are brought before God and you deserve God's wrath, God's anger, God's punishment. But there is One who steps between you and God the Father. He intercedes for you, taking on your punishment, your grief, and your brokenness. He says, "Neither do I condemn you; go and sin no more. Your past has been taken care of." He says, "Father, forgive them, for they know not what they do."

The cross reminds us that Jesus intercedes for us. He steps into our place and goes to the cross for us. A verse from 1 Timothy (2:5-6) puts it this way: "For there is one God; there is also one mediator between God and humankind, Christ Jesus, himself human, who gave himself a ransom for all."

Questions for reflection:

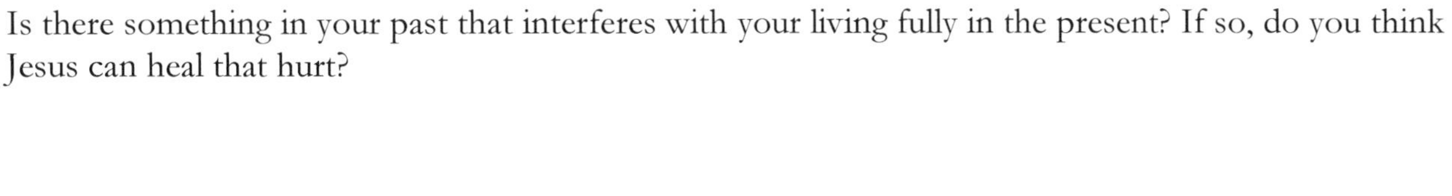

Is there something in your past that interferes with your living fully in the present? If so, do you think Jesus can heal that hurt?

Have you ever experienced an opening up of your future because of an experience of forgiveness? What was it like?

A Psalm for Meditation: *"For as the heavens are high above the earth, so great is his steadfast love toward those who fear him; as far as the east is from the west, so far he removes our transgressions from us. As a father has compassion for his children, so the LORD has compassion for those who fear him."* (Psalm 103:11-13)

Day 4: God of the Second Chance

> ***Luke 7:36-50*** *One of the Pharisees asked Jesus to eat with him, and he went into the Pharisee's house and took his place at the table. [37]And a woman in the city, who was a sinner, having learned that he was eating in the Pharisee's house, brought an alabaster jar of ointment. [38]She stood behind him at his feet, weeping, and began to bathe his feet with her tears and to dry them with her hair. Then she continued kissing his feet and anointing them with the ointment. [39]Now when the Pharisee who had invited him saw it, he said to himself, "If this man were a prophet, he would have known who and what kind of woman this is who is touching him – that she is a sinner." [40]Jesus spoke up and said to him, "Simon, I have something to say to you." "Teacher," he replied, "Speak." [41]"A certain creditor had two debtors; one owed five hundred denarii, and the other fifty. [42]When they could not pay, he canceled the debts for both of them. Now which of them will love him more?"*
>
> *[43]Simon answered, "I suppose the one for whom he canceled the greater debt." And Jesus said to him, "You have judged rightly." [44]Then turning toward the woman, he said to Simon, "Do you see this woman? I entered your house; you gave me no water for my feet, but she has bathed my feet with her tears and dried them with her hair. [45]You gave me no kiss, but from the time I came in she has not stopped kissing my feet. [46]You did not anoint my head with oil, but she has anointed my feet with ointment. [47]Therefore, I tell you, her sins, which were many, have been forgiven; hence she has shown great love. But the one to whom little is forgiven, loves little." [48]Then he said to her, "Your sins are forgiven." [49]But those who were at the table with him began to say among themselves, "Who is this who even forgives sins?" [50]And he said to the woman, "Your faith has saved you; go in peace."*

I would think that after a few of these dinners, the word would be out: Be careful about inviting Jesus to your house for dinner. There's no telling what he might say or do. Simon, however, had to learn this the hard way. Jesus has accepted a dinner invitation at the house of Simon, a Pharisee. While they are reclining at the table, a woman comes into the room. The woman is an uninvited guest. In that day it seems doors and windows remained open, and people wandered in.

This woman has a bad reputation. She has come to this house because she has heard that Jesus is there. But when she finds herself in his presence, "she is overcome, and his feet are wet with her tears before she can get the ointment jar open. Then, trying to make things better, she makes them worse as far as the onlookers are concerned;" having nothing else with which to dry his feet, "she lets down her hair, something no decent woman would do in public," and wipes his feet with her hair and kisses his feet while drying them. And finally she anoints his feet with her ointment.[64]

At first Simon is embarrassed to have her in his house. Everyone knows what kind of woman she is. But then he is indignant because Jesus does not seem to know what kind of woman she is. Doesn't he recognize a prostitute when he sees one? If he were really an upright man of God, if he were really a prophet he would not allow her to touch him in that way.

Questions for reflection:

Do you think that it was an oversight or do you think Simon did not want to humble himself to show hospitality to Jesus?

Simon is embarrassed to have this woman in his house. The woman is likely embarrassed about her emotional reaction to being in Jesus' presence (in addition to the embarrassment about her own identity). Only Jesus does not seem to be embarrassed, even at the way the woman is touching him. Why is that?

Prayer: *God of the second chance, thank you for your grace that forgives us and releases us from past failures and broken promises. Like the woman who stands accused, let us hear your reassuring words that you do not condemn us, but you give us a new, open future. Amen.*

Day 5: Forgiveness and Love

There's an obvious difference between Jesus and Simon. "Here are two religious leaders suddenly in the presence of a sinful woman. One has an understanding of righteousness which causes him to distance himself from her; the other understands righteousness to mean moving toward her with forgiveness and a blessing of peace."[65]

Jesus notices Simon's disapproval and proceeds to tell a story. A parable. A certain creditor had two debtors. One owed $100,000, and the other owed $10,000. Neither could pay back his debt, so the creditor canceled both of their debts. Now which of them will love him more? Simon answers, "The one who owed him the greater debt." That's right, Simon. Now, do you see this woman? When I entered your house, you did not extend to me the customary courtesies of hospitality. You did not provide me with water to wash my feet, but she has bathed my feet with her tears and dried them with her hair. You did not give me a kiss of welcome, but she has not stopped kissing my feet. You did not anoint my head with oil, but she has anointed my feet with her ointment. Although you are the host, it is this woman who has extended a lavish hospitality. She is like the one in the story that was forgiven the greater debt, and her gratitude and her love are signs of that forgiveness.

Jesus is saying that the woman's behavior demonstrates a love that comes from her being forgiven. (The greater the cancelled debt, the greater the love.) Simon's neglect, on the other hand, shows that grace hasn't penetrated his life. The woman is well aware of her sinfulness and her need for forgiveness. Simon does not recognize that his self-righteous pride could be as serious a sin as anything the sinful woman has done. Both Simon and the woman are in need of God's forgiveness. The difference is that she knows it and receives it, while Simon does not.

Questions for reflection:

Is it easier to see the sins of others or your own sins? How would Simon answer this question? How about the woman?

Jesus seems to be saying that God's grace works in a person's life and causes the person to become more gracious (and loving). How have you seen this played out in your life or in the lives of others?

Day 6: Forgiveness of Others

> ***1 Peter 4:8*** *"Above all, maintain constant love for one another, for love covers a multitude of sins."*

Love covers a multitude of sins. When we are immersed in God's love, when we are saturated with God's forgiveness and grace, we will be drawn to share that grace and forgiveness with others. That's how we are to understand that petition of the Lord's Prayer: "forgive us our trespasses as we forgive those who trespass against us." As Martin Luther teaches, this petition reminds us that none of us is more righteous than anyone else, "that in the presence of God all people must fall on their knees and be glad that we can come to forgiveness."[66] Our willingness to forgive others is linked to our acceptance that we are all sinners in need of forgiveness.

There is an interrelatedness between the forgiveness we receive from God and the forgiveness we are to extend to others. In other words, if we choose not to forgive, but to harbor bitterness in our hearts, we deny ourselves the gift of forgiveness from God. Some people are bitter people because they have become stuck spiritually; an unforgiving spirit has led them to live under the cloud of bitterness.

One danger of not forgiving is that we will become trapped or imprisoned in bitterness. That we will live in the past rather than live the new, abundant life God gives us in Christ.

Forgiveness is different from reconciliation in that it does not require two people. Sometimes forgiveness can be experienced between two people where both people are intentional about it. There are other times when you can forgive another person, even without the other person being aware of it, even when the other person may not have asked for it or desired it. Forgiveness in that sense is your decision to leave the past in the past and to move on. Whether or not the other person actively participates in the process, you don't need to remain in bitterness, or sacrifice your ability to live in God's blessing.

As Christians we stand on the grace of God, and we believe in God's remarkable power to redeem people from their past, and to set them free into a wide open future to live the new life which God gives in Jesus Christ.

Questions for reflection:

Having received the forgiveness of God in the depths of your life, how has it overflowed from you to others?

Sometimes we may not know the exact time when we have forgiven another person. But at some point, we realize that the deep angry feelings have been released, and we do not react with strong emotions when a memory comes to mind. We may even find ourselves praying for the person and wishing the person well. Dietrich Bonhoeffer teaches us that we cannot pray for a person very long without moving toward forgiving them. It is in prayer that we come to see the other person through the eyes of Jesus. Is there someone you need to forgive? Are you praying for that person?

Taking It Further: Small Group and Chapter Summary Questions

How can forgiveness open up the future?

In what situations might forgiveness not include reconciliation between two people?

If God's grace has a power to work grace in us, how do you explain the possibility of being forgiven yourself and not forgiving others?

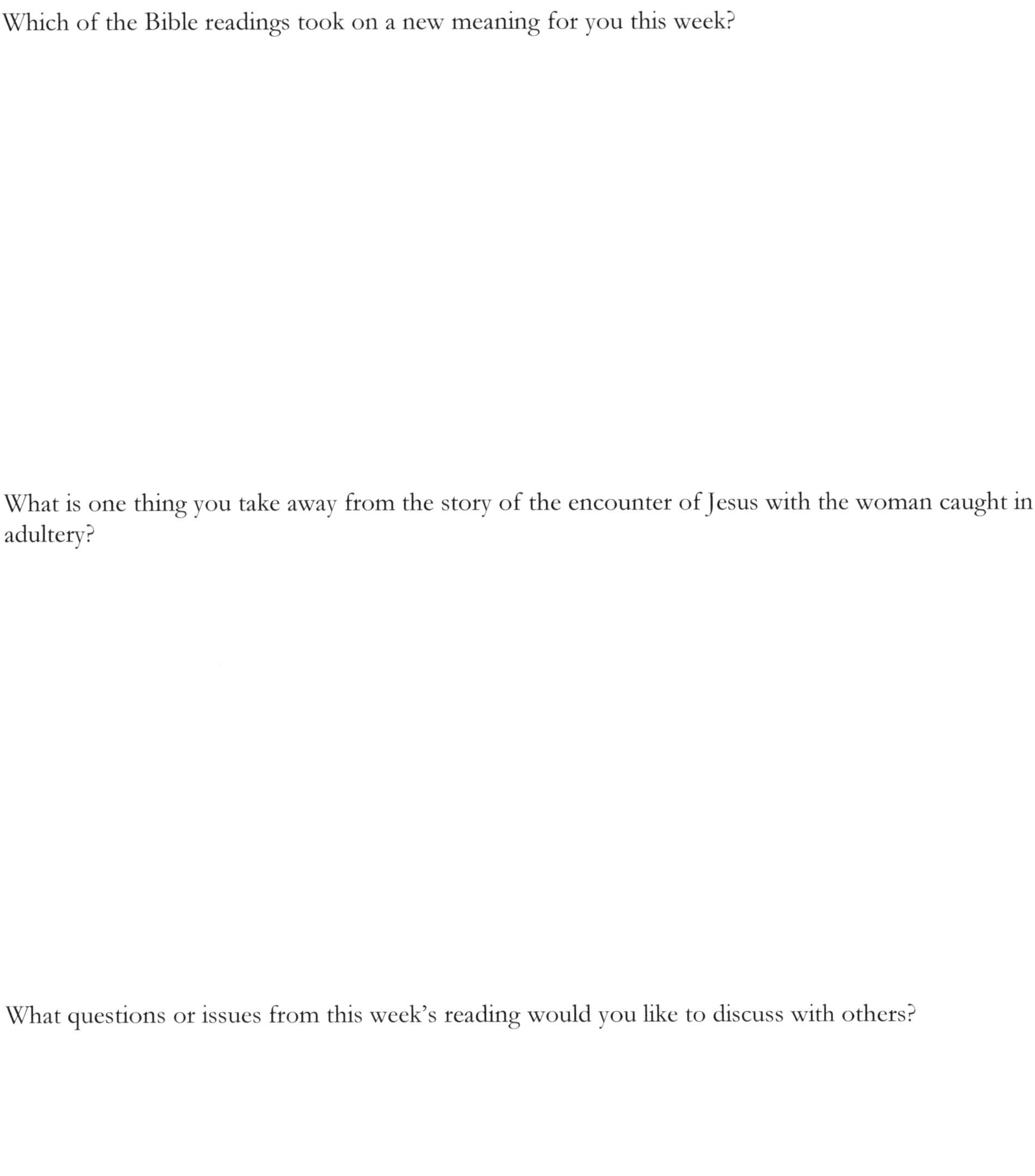

Which of the Bible readings took on a new meaning for you this week?

What is one thing you take away from the story of the encounter of Jesus with the woman caught in adultery?

What questions or issues from this week's reading would you like to discuss with others?

How was your relationship to God deepened this week?

Recommended resources for further study:

Kenneth Bailey, *Jesus Through Middle Eastern Eyes; Cultural Studies in the Gospels*

Liz Curtis Higgs, *Really Bad Girls of the Bible: More Lessons from Less-Than-Perfect-Women*

Chapter Eight: Restored

Day 1: Simon the Rock

When his brother Andrew introduced Simon to Jesus, Jesus gave him a new name, Cephas, (the Aramaic word for rock), which in New Testament Greek, becomes Peter (John 1:42). "He would eventually become the 'rock' of the church, but only after a long arduous journey with many stumbles and falls."[67] That's why we like Peter so much…we identify both with his steps forward and his missteps. Our gospel readings this week tell about God's work of restoration in the life of Peter.

According to the gospels, Peter was among the first disciples to leave it all and follow Jesus.

> ***Matthew 4:18-20*** *As he walked by the Sea of Galilee, he saw two brothers, Simon, who is called Peter, and Andrew his brother, casting a net into the sea – for they were fishermen. [19]And he said to them, "Follow me, and I will make you fish for people." [20]Immediately they left their nets and followed him.*

Peter and the other disciples traveled with Jesus to towns and villages, visiting the local synagogues on the Sabbath. They watched Jesus teach and preach along the way. They saw him heal people and cast out demons. They heard Jesus tell parables, and get involved in debates with the religious leaders.

Luke's gospel expands on the story in which Peter left the fishing boats to follow Jesus.

> ***Luke 5:1-11*** *Once while Jesus was standing beside the lake of Gennesaret, and the crowd was pressing in on him to hear the word of God, [2]he saw two boats there at the shore of the lake; the fishermen had gone out of them and were washing their nets. [3]He got into one of the boats, the one belonging to Simon, and asked him to put out a little way from the shore. Then he sat down and taught the crowds from the boat. [4]When he had finished speaking, he said to Simon, "Put out into the deep water and let down your nets for a catch." [5]Simon answered, "Master, we have worked all night long but have caught nothing. Yet if you say so, I will let down the nets." [6]When they had done this, they caught so many fish that their nets were beginning to break. [7]So they signaled their partners in the other boat to come and help them. And they came and filled both boats, so that they began to sink. [8]But when Simon Peter saw it, he fell down at Jesus' knees, saying, "Go away from me, Lord, for I am a sinful man!" [9]For he and all who were with him were amazed at the catch of fish that they had taken; [10]and so also were James and John, sons of Zebedee, who were partners with Simon. Then Jesus said to Simon, "Do not be afraid; from now on you will be catching people." [11]When they had brought their boats to shore, they left everything and followed him.*

The miraculous catch of fish catches Peter's attention. He perceives that he is in the presence of someone very special…someone he calls, "Lord." And like Isaiah's vision of God in the temple (Isaiah 6:1-6), Peter immediately recognizes his own unworthiness to stand in the presence of Jesus. He falls to his knees and cries out: "Go away from me, Lord, for I am a sinful man!"

Questions for reflection:

What does Jesus mean that Peter and the others will be "catching people" in a similar way to the miraculous catch of fish?

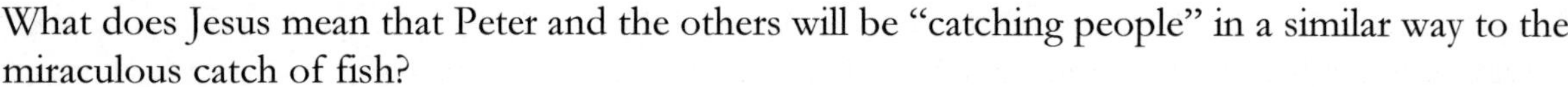

What do you think Peter sees in Jesus, that both causes him to be aware of his own sinfulness, and leads him to leave everything to follow Jesus?

Day 2: A Difficult Walk

One stormy night, the disciples are in a boat on the lake, and they see Jesus walking toward them on the water. Peter's faith leads him to venture out on the water with Jesus. But soon he focuses on the wind and the waves rather than on Jesus, and he sinks (like a rock). Jesus grabs him and pulls him into the boat, saying "O man of little faith, why did you doubt?" (Matthew 14:23-33)

Not long thereafter Jesus and his disciples are walking on the way to Caesarea Philippi when Jesus asks them, "Who do people say that I am?" They tell him what they have heard (John the Baptist, one of the prophets, or Elijah). And then Jesus asks them directly: Who do you say that I am? Peter (who often seems to be the spokesman for the group) answers for the rest "You are the Christ. You are God's Messiah."

> ***Matthew 16:17-23*** *- And Jesus answered him, "Blessed are you, Simon son of*
> *Jonah! For flesh and blood has not revealed this to you, but my Father in heaven.*
> *18 And I tell you, you are Peter, and on this rock I will build my church, and the gates*
> *of Hades will not prevail against it. 19 I will give you the keys of the kingdom of*
> *heaven, and whatever you bind on earth will be bound in heaven, and whatever you*
> *loose on earth will be loosed in heaven." 20 Then he sternly ordered the disciples not*
> *to tell anyone that he was the Messiah. 21 From that time on, Jesus began to show his*
> *disciples that he must go to Jerusalem and undergo great suffering at the hands of*
> *the elders and chief priests and scribes, and be killed, and on the third day be raised.*
> *22 And Peter took him aside and began to rebuke him, saying, "God forbid it, Lord!*
> *This must never happen to you." 23 But he turned and said to Peter, "Get behind me,*
> *Satan! You are a stumbling block to me; for you are setting your mind not on divine*
> *things but on human things."*

Jesus affirms Peter's confession, calling it a divine revelation. However, when Jesus begins to teach the disciples why they are heading for Jerusalem (his coming crucifixion), Peter will hear none of it. He speaks up: "Jesus, this shall never happen to you." Jesus hears in the words of Peter a satanic temptation to draw him away from the Father's will, (away from the cross), and he confronts Peter about his misguided efforts to protect Jesus.

How quickly Peter moves from a "divine" confession of faith in Jesus to a "satanic" opposition to the purpose of God. Isn't that often the way it happens? Just when we think we have mastered some flaw or reached a new "spiritual depth," our humanity shows itself in some embarrassing way

Questions for reflection:

Peter almost gets it right. He can walk on water for a moment. But then he falls. Do you see any resemblance in your own life?

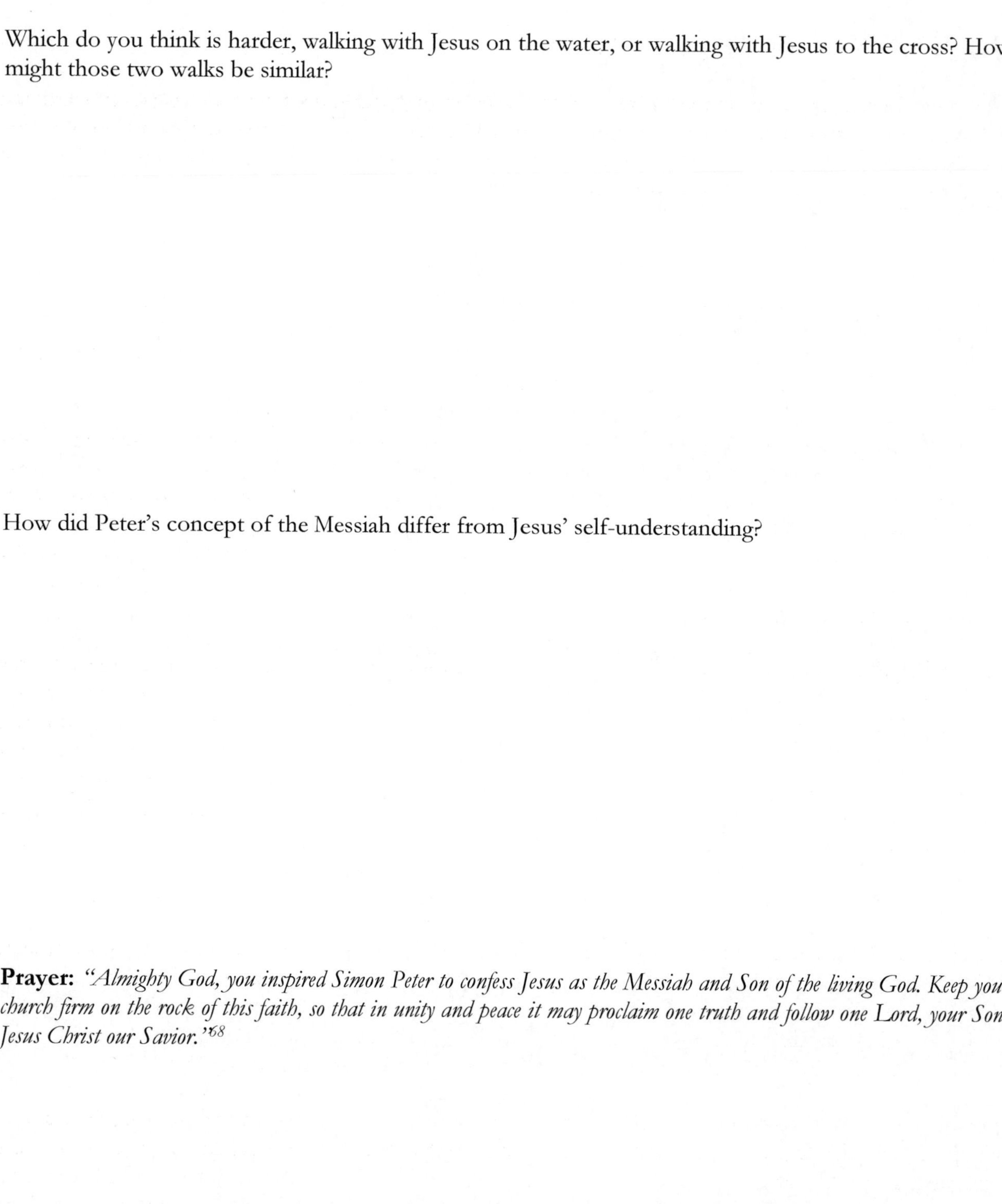

Which do you think is harder, walking with Jesus on the water, or walking with Jesus to the cross? How might those two walks be similar?

How did Peter's concept of the Messiah differ from Jesus' self-understanding?

Prayer: *"Almighty God, you inspired Simon Peter to confess Jesus as the Messiah and Son of the living God. Keep your church firm on the rock of this faith, so that in unity and peace it may proclaim one truth and follow one Lord, your Son, Jesus Christ our Savior."*[68]

Day 3: A Mixture of Pride and Humility

At the meal we call the last supper, Jesus picks up a basin of water and a towel and begins to wash and dry the feet of his disciples. We're not surprised that Peter is the one who objects to his Lord washing his feet. "You, Lord, wash my feet? You shall never wash my feet." But Jesus responds, "If I do not wash you, you will not be in fellowship with me."

"Oh," says Peter, "if that is what you mean, then wash all of me."

"Your feet will be enough, Peter." (John 13:6-10 paraphrase)

"Peter was humble enough to feel that his Lord should not perform such menial service on him, but too proud to remain quiet and learn a valuable lesson."[69]

That same night, Jesus warns his friends that they will all abandon him. Guess who speaks up? Peter protests: "Everyone else may fall away, but I never will. I will follow you until death." And Jesus responds: I tell you, tonight before the cock crows you will disown me three times. Once again we see in Peter's heart that mixture of sincere love for Jesus and his own ignorance "that overestimates both his own grasp of the situation and underestimates his own capacity for cowardice."[70] Later in the Garden of Gethsemane we see this play out again when the disciples are unable to pray and wait with Jesus ("the spirit indeed is willing, but the flesh is weak" - Mark 14:38).

They take Jesus away, and Peter follows, at a safe distance, to watch what would happen. In the courtyard, a maid confronts Peter and accuses him of being friends with Jesus the Galilean. He responds: "I do not know the man." A little later, someone else says to him: You also are one of them, but Peter denies it: "I am not." Soon another is insisting, surely this man was with him; for he is a Galilean, but Peter responds: "Man, I do not know what you are talking about!" While he is speaking, he hears the cock crow, and Jesus turns and looks at Peter, and Peter remembers his words and he goes away tears pouring down his face, like rain on a rock.

Meditation (Nancy Schmitz)

I know that Peter's action of drawing his sword in the Garden of Gethsemane is typically portrayed as rash and impulsive, one more example of his flawed character, but I see it as brave. In that decision to draw his sword and strike he had to know it would mean his own death, but at that moment he chose faithfulness in defending his Lord over security and fleeing. He knew with certainty Jesus' words before he spoke them: "all who draw the sword will die by the sword," and yet he still drew it.

The heart of the issue was not that he was rash, but that he was opposing the will of God, the same as his tête-à-tête with Jesus at Caesarea Philippi. Even moments later when he did flee with the rest of the disciples, he could not entirely desert his Lord, and he followed at a distance. Yes, he did deny him three times, but who else of the disciples was even there to be challenged, except John, and he apparently escaped questioning. If it were me, I never would have made it to the courtyard, and isn't that as much a denial of Christ as Peter's?

Questions for reflection:

What might you draw from Paul's words to explain some of Peter's behavior?

> ***Romans 7:19-25*** *For I do not do the good I want, but the evil I do not want is what I do. [20]Now if I do what I do not want, it is no longer I that do it, but sin that dwells within me. [21]So I find it to be a law that when I want to do what is good, evil lies close at hand. [22]For I delight in the law of God in my inmost self, [23]but I see in my members another law at war with the law of my mind, making me captive to the law of sin that dwells in my members. [24]Wretched man that I am! Who will rescue me from this body of death? [25]Thanks be to God through Jesus Christ our Lord!*

Day 4: Do You Love Me?

Jesus was arrested, beaten, tried, and crucified, all in a little over twelve hours. Something extraordinary happened two days later!! The One who had been crucified was making appearances to his followers!! He was alive, but in a somewhat different way. One of those appearances involved a breakfast on the beach and a conversation between Jesus and Peter. "Three times in the courtyard, Peter faced questions of his relationship to Jesus. Three times he answered no. Three times by the lakeshore, Peter faces questions of his love for Jesus. Three times he answers yes."[71]

> ***John 21:15-17*** *When they had finished breakfast, Jesus said to Simon Peter, "Simon*
> *son of John, do you love me more than these?" He said to him, "Yes, Lord; you*
> *know that I love you." Jesus said to him, "Feed my lambs." [16]A second time he said*
> *to him, "Simon son of John, do you love me?" He said to him, "Yes, Lord; you know*
> *that I love you." Jesus said to him, "Tend my sheep." [17]He said to him the third time,*
> *"Simon son of John, do you love me?" Peter felt hurt because he said to him the*
> *third time, "Do you love me?" And he said to him, "Lord, you know everything; you*
> *know that I love you." Jesus said to him, "Feed my sheep.*

Simon, son of John (like our mother calling us by our full name) do you love me? (Jesus uses Peter's name Simon, as if he's starting over with Peter, giving Peter another chance. And once again He invites Peter to follow him.) Do you really love me more than these other disciples do? (Remember that Peter vowed although the others might let Jesus down, Peter never would.) Do you love me with your whole heart, soul, mind, and strength? Feed my lambs. I am appointing you, Peter, to leadership among my people. Peter is restored to his relationship with Jesus and given a wide open future. Peter, the one who often does and says the wrong things, will be leader of God's people, the rock on which Jesus builds his church.

Through the ordeal of Jesus' passion, Peter discovers his own frailty, his own weakness. He now understands that his ministry will need to be based on God's grace, not on his own courage or strength or wisdom.

God loves the work of restoration. God loves to take a flawed creature, like Peter, and refashion him into a new life formed through grace. God, through his love and forgiveness, seeks to reshape broken lives and restore them to wide open futures. Marriages that are falling apart, lives that are trapped in the past, successful people that are running on empty…Nothing, no one, is considered unsalvageable by God. There is the potential of God's work of restoration in every life

Questions for reflection:

What does Peter learn about relying on his own effort and strength? What have you learned about that?

In what ways might a follower of Jesus deny Jesus today?

Describe a life crisis that drew you closer to God.

Prayer: *"God of our heart and soul and mind and strength, we know that your desire is for us to give ourselves in love entirely to you, but it can be a difficult task. We would give you all we own, except that our wealth represents our security. We would give you our time, except there are so many things that seem to need our attention…We would give you our fears, except then we would have to live courageously…Therefore, God, we can only give you our 'except that's' and offer our love to you piecemeal, as we are able. Please gather up our fragmented lives into your healing embrace. Allow our yearning for wholeness and integrity to overcome whatever barriers we have erected between ourselves and you. Help us to trust you more fully each day. Amen."*[72]

Day 5: Peter the Leader

> ***Luke 22:31-32*** *Simon, Simon, listen! Satan has demanded to sift all of you like wheat, [32]but I have prayed for you that your own faith may not fail; and you, when once you have turned back, strengthen your brothers."*

In Luke's version of the Passover meal, the meal we have come to call the "last supper," Jesus turns to Peter and says: "Peter, listen: Satan has tried and is trying to separate all of you from me, like chaff from wheat. But I have prayed for you that your faith uphold you. And when you turn back to me, strengthen your brothers."

Peter has no idea of what Jesus is talking about; he cannot imagine that he would ever turn away from Jesus. And so he boldly says, "Lord I am ready to go with you to prison and even to death!" But Jesus brings him back down to earth: "Peter, before the rooster crows you will have denied three times that you know me."

It happened as Jesus said. As Jesus is on trial before Pontius Pilate, outside in the courtyard, Peter also faces a kind of trial. He is accused by three persons of being a follower of Jesus, and each time he denies knowing his Lord. And then Peter hears the rooster crowing, and he remembers the words of Jesus, and he goes away, weeping in deep sorrow. Peter the Denier. Peter the Coward. Peter, who said he was ready to die with Jesus, shows that he's not so brave after all.

What is most interesting about this conversation between Jesus and Peter is this statement of Jesus, (You who are about to deny me,) "When you turn back to me, strengthen your brothers." Do you see it? In the context of the story, Jesus has forgiven Peter for denying him, even before Peter has committed the act. Jesus has already forgiven Peter and has given him the role of leader to encourage and support the rest of the disciples.

According to Jesus, Peter is not Peter the Denier or Peter the Coward. Jesus does not look at Peter that way. Jesus sees Peter as the forgiven one. He sees Peter as an encourager of others. (As we read yesterday in John 21:15-17, while Jesus and the disciples are having breakfast by the shore, Jesus asks Peter a question three times, one for each denial: Peter, do you love me? Yes, Lord, you know that I love you. Take care of my sheep.) Peter becomes Peter the Shepherd. Peter the leader. Peter the Rock. God is in the name-changing business. Even more than that…God is in the life-changing business.

Questions for reflection:

Is there a name (that you have been called) that you want God to change? Why don't you pray about it now?

Is there a disappointment about yourself or your life that is hard to get over? Make it a matter of prayer.

Day 6: A New Name

> ***Isaiah 62:1-5 -*** *For Zion's sake I will not keep silent, and for Jerusalem's sake I will not rest, until her vindication shines out like the dawn, and her salvation like a burning torch.* [2]*The nations shall see your vindication, and all the kings your glory; and you shall be called by a new name that the mouth of the LORD will give.* [3]*You shall be a crown of beauty in the hand of the LORD, and a royal diadem in the hand of your God.* [4]*You shall no more be termed Forsaken, and your land shall no more be termed Desolate; but you shall be called My Delight Is in Her, and your land Married; for the LORD delights in you, and your land shall be married.* [5]*For as a young man marries a young woman, so shall your builder marry you, and as the bridegroom rejoices over the bride, so shall your God rejoice over you.*

Rick & Patty White appeared in a foreign court a few years ago to adopt a little girl named Olona. "With about two years of background to the proceeding, they stood with her as a judge read from a document that said such things as 'Inasmuch as Olona Morgan is orphaned and unwanted by any family in this country,' and 'Inasmuch as no citizen of this country wishes to have Olona Morgan.' At the end of that awful recitation, which transferred a little girl from state custody to Rick and Patty White, they dropped to their knees, embraced her, and promised, 'You will never hear the word "unwanted" spoken of you again.' That little girl is thriving in her new home now and –at her own initiative and request – has now changed her name from Olona Morgan to Hope White!"[73]

Long ago, the people of Israel returned home from exile in Babylon only to find themselves still oppressed and poor and their city, Jerusalem, in ruins. The return home was a huge disappointment. Famine and poverty were rampant. The land was desolate. It seemed that the Lord had forsaken his people. Israel was rejected and ruined. The people had no hope. Into this great doubt and discouragement, the prophet Isaiah speaks an encouraging word of hope: God will not give up on you, Israel. God's love endures forever. "You shall be called by a new name that the mouth of the LORD will give... You shall no more be termed *Forsaken*, (and your land shall no more be termed *Desolate*;) but you shall be called *My Delight Is in Her*...for the LORD delights in you... as the bridegroom rejoices over the bride, so shall your God rejoice over you. "Israel," Isaiah proclaims, "You will never hear the word 'forsaken' spoken of you again."

In one of Beth Moore's sessions from her *Believing God* DVD Bible Study, she had 11 or 12 women put on jackets that were each labeled with some reproach, a name that identified some stigma or disgrace. Names like divorced, shamed, crazy, bankrupt, fired, terrible parent, pregnant outside marriage, harlot, DWI, and unwanted.

Perhaps you can identify with one of those names? Perhaps you have carried one of those names around for some years, and it has even become part of your identity? Have you continued to live with a name that brings you down? A name imposed by others or even self-selected which weighs you down and continues to sap your life? Failure? Addict? Drop-Out? Unemployed? It's time to drop that name.

Isaiah tells Israel: you shall no longer be called *Forsaken*. You shall be called *God's delight*. Rick and Patty White kneel down and tell their new daughter Olona, "You will never hear the word 'unwanted' spoken of you again." God's word to you today is the same word. You are beloved. You are the one in whom God delights. That other name you have been carrying around...It is no longer true, if it ever was.

Something happened long ago that also continues to happen in human lives today. Death and resurrection. Cross and new life. In Jesus Christ, God takes your old name, and gives you a new name, and a new life. In Jesus, you have a new name. God's delight. One blessed by God. Receive a new name God wants to give you in Jesus: The one God loves.

Questions for reflection:

Do you know that you are "the one God loves?" How do you feel about that?

What area of your life could use some of God's restoration work? Let this be a matter of prayer.

Prayer: *Like Peter, Lord, I have good intentions. I want to love you and serve you with all my heart. I want to live for you and with you each day. But then I fail to trust you. Or I misunderstand where you are going and what you ask of me. And I live as if I did not know you. May I hear your word of grace anew each day, that I am the one God loves. Amen.*

Taking It Further: Small Group and Chapter Summary Questions

What do you most appreciate about the story of Peter's life from the gospels (or later from the Acts of the Apostles)?

What events in Peter's life do you find similar to your own life?

What does Peter learn about the grace of the Lord?

What works of God's restoration have you observed?

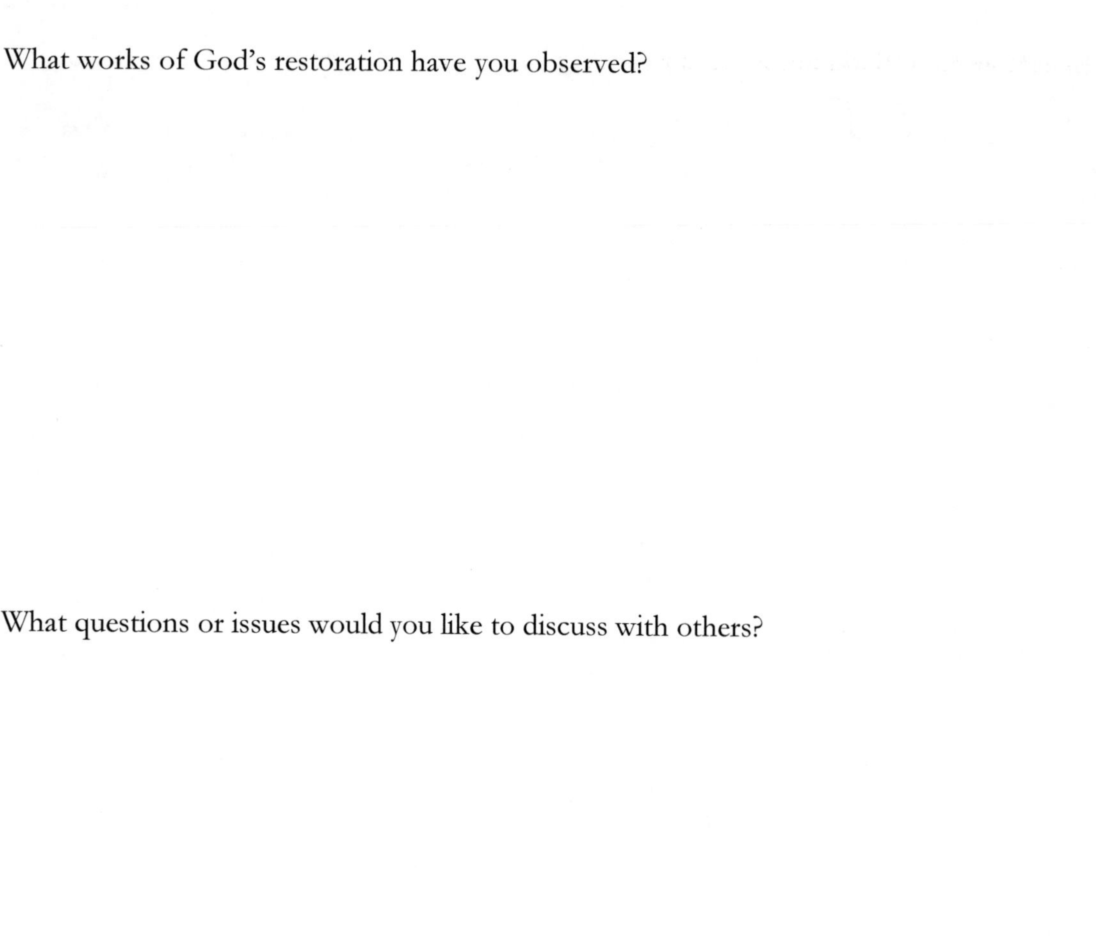

What questions or issues would you like to discuss with others?

Which of the Bible readings took on a new meaning for you this week?

How was your relationship to God deepened this week?

What do you want to remember from this chapter?

Recommended resources for further study:

Kenneth Bailey, *Jesus Through Middle Eastern Eyes: Cultural Studies in the Gospels*

Chapter Nine: The One Thing

Day 1: Do You Know What You Are Asking?

> ***Luke 9:57-62*** *And as they were going along the road, someone said to Him, "I will follow You wherever You go."* [58]*And Jesus said to him, "The foxes have holes, and the birds of the air have nests, but the Son of Man has nowhere to lay His head."* [59]*And He said to another, "Follow Me." But he said, "Permit me first to go and bury my father."* [60]*But He said to him, "Allow the dead to bury their own dead; but as for you, go and proclaim everywhere the kingdom of God."* [61]*And another also said, "I will follow You, Lord; but first permit me to say good-bye to those at home."* [62]*But Jesus said to him, "No one, after putting his hand to the plow and looking back, is fit for the kingdom of God."*

In Luke 9:51 and following, Jesus is resolutely determined – he is on his way to Jerusalem, and will not be diverted from that purpose. There he will suffer, be rejected, and be crucified. The ministry of Jesus is attracting potential followers. Someone comes up to Jesus and volunteers: "I will follow you wherever you go." The man enthusiastically volunteers to join Jesus on his journey. You would think that that is the kind of follower Jesus is looking for. Someone who steps forward with enthusiasm and passion and volunteers. But how does Jesus respond? 9:58 – "Foxes have dens and birds have nests, but the Son of Man has nowhere to rest his head."

What is Jesus saying? My kingdom is not what you think it is. Even the animals have places to call home, places to rest. But I am totally dependent on the hospitality of others. Are you sure you want to come along? Are you willing to put yourself in such a place? You don't know where I am going. How can you say you will follow me? The would-be follower has no idea that the journey leads to Gethsemane, Golgotha and a tomb. So Jesus bids the man count the cost, to realize what he is getting into before he promises that he will follow Jesus anywhere he goes.

Otherwise, the would-be follower would be like the young man who wrote this note to his girlfriend,

Dear Mary,

I love you so much. I would swim the deepest ocean for you.
I would climb the highest mountain for you.
I would walk the highest desert just to see you.
P.S. I'll be over Saturday night, if it doesn't rain.

Questions for reflection:

Why would Jesus discourage someone from following him?

What do you think it means to follow Jesus to Jerusalem?

What connections do you see between Jesus' words in Luke 9:57-62 (above) and his words in Luke 14:28-30?

> ***Luke 14:28-30*** *"For which of you, intending to build a tower, does not first sit down and estimate the cost, to see whether he has enough to complete it?* [29]*Otherwise, when he has laid a foundation and is not able to finish, all who see it will begin to ridicule him,* [30]*saying, 'This fellow began to build and was not able to finish.'"*

Prayer: *Lord God, so draw my heart to you, so guide my mind, so fill my imagination, so control my will, that I may be wholly yours, utterly dedicated to you; and then use me, I pray, as you will, but always to your glory and the welfare of your people, through my Lord and Savior, Jesus Christ. Amen.*[74]

Day 2: I Will Follow, but First…

> ***Repeat Luke 9:57-62*** *And as they were going along the road, someone said to Him, "I will follow You wherever You go." [58]And Jesus said to him, "The foxes have holes, and the birds of the air have nests, but the Son of Man has nowhere to lay His head." [59]And He said to another, "Follow Me." But he said, "Permit me first to go and bury my father." [60]But He said to him, "Allow the dead to bury their own dead; but as for you, go and proclaim everywhere the kingdom of God." [61]And another also said, "I will follow You, Lord; but first permit me to say good-bye to those at home." [62]But Jesus said to him, "No one, after putting his hand to the plow and looking back, is fit for the kingdom of God."*

There's a second would-be follower. To this one Jesus says, "follow me." And the man responds with a request: "Lord, ***first*** let me go and bury my father" (9:59). That seems like a reasonable request. Surely Jesus will allow this important duty to be done.

But don't think that the man's father has already died and is awaiting burial. If that were the case, the man wouldn't be away from home listening to Jesus. No, the man is referring to the middle eastern way of life in which one is expected to stay home until one has fulfilled the traditional duty of taking care of one's parents until their deaths.[75]

The man is probably thinking, surely you do not expect me to violate the expectations of my community and family? But that is precisely what Jesus expects, as we hear in his shocking reply: "Let the dead bury their own dead; but as for you, go and proclaim the kingdom of God." Let your family take care of the traditional responsibility, but as for you, go and announce the arrival of God's kingdom.

Loyalty to Jesus takes precedence over the highest family obligation. The man assumes that Jesus will honor his family commitments, but he learns that with Jesus, there is one commitment above all others. Whenever one responds, "I will follow, **but first…**" one is putting one's own desires ahead of God's desires, one's own agenda before God's agenda. According to Jesus, there is only one "first," and for Jesus that is God and God's kingdom:

> *But strive **first** for the kingdom of God and his righteousness, and all these things will be given to you as well.* ***(Matthew 6:33)***

Questions for reflection:

Have you ever found yourself saying to Jesus something like one of these replies:

Yes, Jesus, I would like to follow you, but you don't mind if I do it my way?

Yes, Jesus, I would like to follow you, but my schedule will not allow for many interruptions.

I will follow you, but there are a few places that I just will not go.

I will follow, but I have only this time available.

I will follow, but first let me do this.

Which reply hits closest to home? Why?

Day 3: Look Where You Are Going

> ***Repeat Luke 9:57-62*** *And as they were going along the road, someone said to Him, "I will follow You wherever You go." [58]And Jesus said to him, "The foxes have holes, and the birds of the air have nests, but the Son of Man has nowhere to lay His head." [59]And He said to another, "Follow Me." But he said, "Permit me first to go and bury my father." [60]But He said to him, "Allow the dead to bury their own dead; but as for you, go and proclaim everywhere the kingdom of God." [61]And another also said, "I will follow You, Lord; but first permit me to say good-bye to those at home." [62]But Jesus said to him, "No one, after putting his hand to the plow and looking back, is fit for the kingdom of God."*

There is a third would-be follower. He tells Jesus, "I will follow you, Lord, but let me ***first*** say farewell to those at my home." Once again, it seems to us like a reasonable request. But not to Jesus. (And did you notice that word "first" again?) The phrase translated "say goodbye" is better translated "request permission to leave." In other words, the man is asking to go home and get permission from his father. (And it's very unlikely that the father would allow his son to go off on some questionable journey, so the potential follower has his ready-made excuse.[76]) The man is saying that he must get his father's permission to venture out.

Once again Jesus challenges the request. Jesus claims an authority higher than the man's father. "No one who puts a hand to the plow and looks back is fit for the kingdom of God." (Many of us don't have much experience with plowing, so think instead of driving a car. What happens when you look too long in the rear view mirror, or are trying to read a map while driving, or trying to answer a call on your cell phone, or are looking out the window at something along the road? You may hear your tires hitting the shoulder or bumper strips, and find that you have strayed over the line and you need to put your car back on course.)

In the same way, you cannot plow a straight line if you're looking behind yourself. You have to be looking forward. (You have to concentrate on what you're doing.)

This man also assumes that Jesus will respect his loyalty to his family. (After all, isn't family first?) But Jesus tells him: "No one who puts a hand to the plow and looks back is fit for the kingdom of God."

How would you paraphrase Jesus' response in your own words?

Three people were ready to follow Jesus. Their requests are only what we would expect of good, decent people. And yet they are challenged by Jesus, who tells them that they don't fully understand what he expects of them. Jesus raises the bar of discipleship and makes it harder for them. Why? Because it is our natural human tendency to simply add discipleship to our list of duties and values. Jesus teaches that living for God is not merely another commitment we add to our long list, but it is THE COMMITMENT which demands a reordering of everything else. (When Jesus calls you into his life, there comes a reordering of every other concern and commitment.)

Questions for reflection:

What do you think happened to those three people? Did the challenge from Jesus make them more serious about following him, or did they walk away, because Jesus was asking too much? Did the sharp words of Jesus provide for them what they needed to step off of the fence, to step over the line, and commit themselves to him, or did they walk away because they thought they could never measure up?

To what areas of your life is Jesus' call most challenging?
(Family…work…money…security…schedule…self-sufficiency…etc.?)

Thought for meditation:

Sometimes we think that if we lived back then, if we were contemporaries of Jesus, and we heard him teach and saw him heal, we would have followed him unquestioningly. Sometimes we think that the contemporaries of Jesus had an advantage when it comes to faith.

But actually, it's the other way around. They were living the story without knowing the ending. We already know the ending. We already know that the One who asks for our life, has given his life for us. We already know that the One who asks us to give up our agenda gave up his agenda completely, to do the Father's will. We already know that the One who asks for all our heart and mind and strength, has given all his strength and love, his body and blood for us. And when we realize that, how else would we respond?

Day 4: How Can I Find Life?

> ***Matthew 19:16-22*** *- Then someone came to him and said, "Teacher, what good deed must I do to have eternal life?"* [17]*And he said to him, "Why do you ask me about what is good? There is only one who is good. If you wish to enter into life, keep the commandments."* [18]*He said to him, "Which ones?" And Jesus said, "You shall not murder; You shall not commit adultery; You shall not steal; You shall not bear false witness;* [19]*Honor your father and mother; also, You shall love your neighbor as yourself."* [20]*The young man said to him, "I have kept all these; what do I still lack?"* [21]*Jesus said to him, "If you wish to be perfect, go, sell your possessions, and give the money to the poor, and you will have treasure in heaven; then come, follow me."* [22]*When the young man heard this word, he went away grieving, for he had many possessions.*

This gospel reading is a haunting and challenging story. It functions somewhat like a parable, especially for us North Americans, who often take our wealth for granted. The first thing we need to do with this challenging gospel reading is to try to get out of it, right? There must be some way we can soften it a bit… ("Go, sell what you own and give the money to the poor…and then come and follow me.") Surely Jesus didn't mean it the way it sounds, did he?

Maybe the story applies only to those who are wealthy, which means it doesn't apply to us. Many of us may be well off, but we're not *that* wealthy. When Jesus talks about how hard it will be for those who have wealth to enter the kingdom of God, he couldn't mean us? (But we're Americans. And when the rest of the world looks at us, they think we are rich. Most of us own a car. 92% of people in the world do not own a car. More than half the world lives on less than $2 a day. The rest of the world looks at us and thinks "they are rich." So when Jesus is talking about the problem of wealth here in this story, yeah, I think it does apply to most of us.)[77]

Well, then there's always the good ole ninth-century interpretation that refers to a low gate into Jerusalem called "the eye of the needle," through which camels could pass only if on their knees and unburdened. Have you heard this one? In this interpretation, Jesus criticizes those who are not just rich but also proud; they must humble themselves before God. The problem with this interpretation is that no such gate ever existed. This interpretation tries to tone down what is absurd, – the camel, the largest animal (in that region), going through the needle, the smallest opening – to suggest that a rich person, given sufficient humility, might just be able to squeeze in.[78] Jesus uses humor to poke fun at the absurdity of thinking that wealth can do anything about the Age to Come. It's like the joke about never seeing a hearse pulling a U-Haul trailer. Riches can no more help you or go with you into the Age to Come than a camel can go through the eye of a needle.

Questions for reflection:

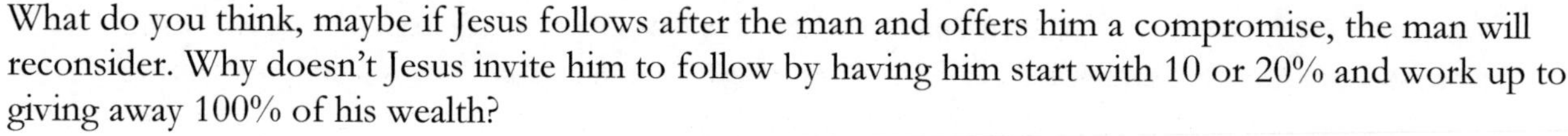

What do you think, maybe if Jesus follows after the man and offers him a compromise, the man will reconsider. Why doesn't Jesus invite him to follow by having him start with 10 or 20% and work up to giving away 100% of his wealth?

Jesus doesn't make it easy on the man. He simply allows the man to choose his life, (to choose his wealth), and to walk away. Why is that?

Day 5: One More Thing

> ***Repeat Matthew 19:16-22*** *- Then someone came to him and said, "Teacher, what*
> *good deed must I do to have eternal life?" 17And he said to him, "Why do you ask me*
> *about what is good? There is only one who is good. If you wish to enter into life,*
> *keep the commandments." 18He said to him, "Which ones?" And Jesus said, "You*
> *shall not murder; You shall not commit adultery; You shall not steal; You shall not*
> *bear false witness; 19Honor your father and mother; also, You shall love your*
> *neighbor as yourself." 20The young man said to him, "I have kept all these; what do*
> *I still lack?" 21Jesus said to him, "If you wish to be perfect, go, sell your possessions,*
> *and give the money to the poor, and you will have treasure in heaven; then come,*
> *follow me." 22When the young man heard this word, he went away grieving, for he*
> *had many possessions.*

Who is the man? Evidently he is rich…he has a lot of possessions. And he seems to be dissatisfied with his life. He's looking for something more. He appears to be sincere; he comes to Jesus looking for "eternal life." Now don't read into this that he's asking about heaven. What he means by "eternal life?" is what we might call "The Age to Come." In Jesus' day, people looked forward to the "Age to Come," when there would be justice and peace, freedom for Israel, punishment for evildoers, the righteous dead would be raised to life, and endless spring would break out all over. (It's what Jesus calls the kingdom of God.) That's in contrast to this "Present Age," which is characterized by sin and injustice, oppression, good people suffering, and wicked people getting away with it. The man suspects that Jesus knows the answer, maybe he even suspects that Jesus is the Messiah, the one who will bring in the Age to Come (the kingdom of God), and so he comes to Jesus with the question.[79]

Jesus points the man to the commandments of God, and the man responds that he has kept the commandments all his life.[80] Now we come to the climax of the encounter. Just how serious is this man? There is one more thing. (Which reminds us of another conversation, when Mary is sitting at Jesus' feet and her sister Martha comes to complain to Jesus that by Mary sitting there, Martha has to do all the work to get the meal ready, And Jesus tells her: "Martha, Martha, you are worried and distracted by many things. There is need of only one thing. Mary has chosen the one thing.")

"You lack one thing; go, sell what you own, and give the money to the poor, and you will have treasure in heaven; then come, follow me." (The man must have stood there, with his mouth hanging open trying to figure out if Jesus was just exaggerating or if he really meant it. WHAT??? Sell *some* things, OK. Give *more* to the poor…he can do that. But *everything*? "That's not reasonable. That's asking too much."[81]

Questions for reflection:

Perhaps his wealth was the man's primary distraction or obsession. What can wealth do for a person? What can it not do?

What is your primary distraction? What is keeping your attention from God?

Day 6: The Cost of Discipleship

> ***Repeat Matthew 19:16-22*** *Then someone came to him and said, "Teacher, what good deed must I do to have eternal life?"* [17]*And he said to him, "Why do you ask me about what is good? There is only one who is good. If you wish to enter into life, keep the commandments."* [18]*He said to him, "Which ones?" And Jesus said, "You shall not murder; You shall not commit adultery; You shall not steal; You shall not bear false witness;* [19]*Honor your father and mother; also, You shall love your neighbor as yourself."* [20]*The young man said to him, "I have kept all these; what do I still lack?"* [21]*Jesus said to him, "If you wish to be perfect, go, sell your possessions, and give the money to the poor, and you will have treasure in heaven; then come, follow me."* [22]*When the young man heard this word, he went away grieving, for he had many possessions.*

Evidently the man is greedy…"and greed has no place in the world to come. He hasn't learned yet that he has a sacred calling to use his wealth to move creation forward… Jesus promises him that if he can do it, if he can trust God to liberate him from his greed, he'll have 'treasure in heaven.' …The man can't do it, and so he walks away."[82]

The man faces a decision: the way of Jesus (giving up his possessions) or his own way (keeping his possessions). His heart is revealed by his response to Jesus' invitation to enter life. The way into the kingdom of God is by following Jesus. And Jesus offers the man that very invitation: "Your life can begin anew right now. It is a question of yes or no, of obedience or disobedience." The man walks away grieving. The decision was just too costly.

We just want to add a little Jesus to the mix of our lives. We want to add Jesus to our life and have everything else remain the same. But Jesus asks for everything. We would prefer to serve two masters, but Jesus calls that an impossibility (Matthew 6:24).

After the man walks away, Jesus summarizes the encounter in these words: "Children, how hard it is to enter the kingdom of God! It is easier for a camel to go through the eye of a needle than for someone who is rich to enter the kingdom of God." The disciples are just as shocked as the rich man, and we are just as shocked as the disciples. Then who can enter God's kingdom? Jesus responds: "For mortals it is impossible, but not for God; for God all things are possible." (In other words, it's not our wealth or our goodness that will get us into the kingdom, but the grace of God alone.)

Questions for reflection:

What connections do you see between this story and Jesus' words in Matthew 6:19-21:

> *Do not store up for yourselves treasures on earth, where moth and rust consume and where thieves break in and steal; but store up for yourselves treasures in heaven, where neither moth nor rust consumes and where thieves do not break in and steal. For where your treasure is, there your heart will be also.*

Jesus calls this man to give up the one thing that he thinks he cannot. What is Jesus calling you to give up in order to follow him?

What do you think about Jesus' words "for mortals it is impossible; but not for God. For God all things are possible."? How is that good news for you?

Prayer: *Forgive us, Lord, when we are unable to say an unqualified "Yes" to your call. "But take our partial 'Yeses.' Take our dim understandings. Take our hesitant faith. Take our half-love. Fan them with the breath of your Spirit that they may lead us more wholeheartedly into submission to your will…Remind us each morning that we may choose anew to move toward life or death, toward wholeness or fragmentation, toward love or meaninglessness. Give us the wisdom and courage we need each day, each hour. Amen."*[83]

In Conclusion

The journey of discipleship is a continual process. We hunger for God; Jesus fills us up with Living Water. We have our own life-changing encounters with Jesus – through prayer, reading the Word, witnessing his miracles in our lives – and through them our faith is born anew. Our eyes are opened. We are forgiven. Restored. We are called to give ourselves over and wholeheartedly follow Jesus. And the journey begins again. We never stop growing, never stop learning, never stop hungering for more.[84]

Taking It Further: Small Group and Chapter Summary Questions

What do you find most challenging about the biblical readings this week?

How has the word of God spoken to you about Jesus' call to follow him?

There's a common saying that Jesus comforts the afflicted, but also afflicts the comfortable. What evidence of this do you see in your own life?

What one thing do you want to remember from your daily reflections this week?

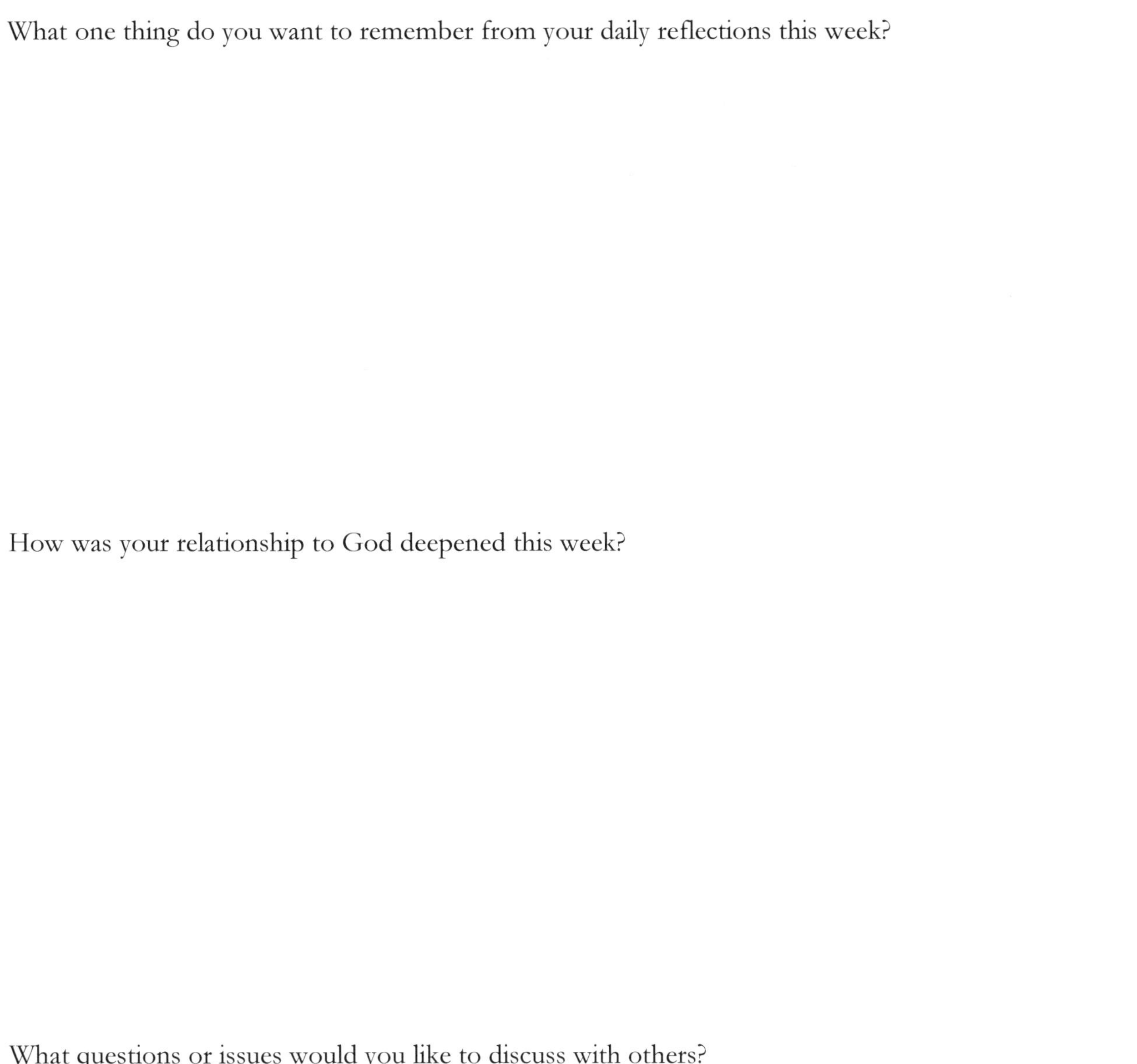

How was your relationship to God deepened this week?

What questions or issues would you like to discuss with others?

Which story, or which encounter with Jesus from this study guide, speaks most personally to your life? Why?

A verse to remember: "But strive first for the kingdom of God and his righteousness, and all these things will be given to you as well." (Matthew 6:33)

Close together by praying this prayer:

Forgive us, Lord, when we are unable to say an unqualified "Yes" to your call. 'But take our partial 'Yes's.' Take our dim understandings. Take our hesitant faith. Take our half-love. Fan them with the breath of your Spirit that they may lead us more wholeheartedly into submission to your will…Remind us each morning that we may choose anew to move toward life or death, toward wholeness or fragmentation, toward love or meaninglessness. Give us the wisdom and courage we need each day, each hour. Amen.'[85]

Recommended resources for further study:

Rob Bell, *Love Wins*

Steven James, *Never the Same: Stories of Those Who Encountered Jesus* N.T. Wright, *Mark for Everyone*

Chapter Ten: Next Steps...

Potential Use in a Worship Series

A Lenten Series

A five week Lenten series about Life-Changing Encounters with Jesus could include chapters 4-8, focusing on Jesus' encounters with Nicodemus, the woman at the well, the blind man, the woman caught in adultery, and Peter. An alternate pattern would be to use chapters 3-7 for the five Sundays of Lent, and conclude the series on Easter with chapter 8 (Peter)

Chapters 4-6 focus on the gospel readings for the second, third, and fourth Sundays of Lent, Year A.

The Rest of the Going Deeper Series

Perhaps you (and your group) would like to continue your study of what it means to follow Jesus? Consider one of the other books of the series, *Going Deeper: A Journey with Jesus.* These five books provide a variety of discipleship studies for small groups and individuals. The books can also be used as curriculum for adult forums and high school Sunday School classes, resources for special worship series, and study guides for church leadership development. Although the sequence of the books is intentional, each book is self-contained and can be used independently from the other books.

God Comes to Us* (Book Two)** Having encountered Christ in book one (Yearning for God***), we desire to learn more about God. This volume makes use of the creeds to introduce the fullness of God as Father, Son, and Holy Spirit, a God who wants to be in relationship with his people.

***Called to Follow* (Book Three)** uses the outline of the baptismal covenant from the *Affirmation of Baptism* service to describe the characteristics of what it means to live as a disciple of Jesus. Christians at all points on their faith journeys will find this to be an in-depth and challenging companion. We learn to live daily, "walking wet," living out our baptism, born anew to become the hands and feet of Christ for the world.

***The Fruit of the Spirit* (Book Four)** studies the fruit of the Spirit, the qualities – the character of Jesus Christ – that the Spirit desires to produce in the church and in individual disciples.

***The Body of Christ* (Book Five)** studies the biblical images of church to present a picture of what it means to be the church today, living among God's people, and sent out into the world. This resource also offers a 12-month set of devotions on leadership for church councils.

Chapter Eleven: Small Group Guidelines

This series, *Going Deeper: A Journey with Jesus,* is intended to be a readily accessible resource for small group use. It does not require a leader's guide, nor extra preparation for small group leaders. For small groups that already have designated leaders, the leaders can facilitate the discussion. Other small groups will be able to use this resource with a shared or a rotational leadership. If you are using this discipleship resource in a small group, please review this chapter as a group at the beginning of your time together.

A good way to begin is to form a small group that agrees to meet together for about 10-12 weeks. This approach assumes that the group will complete almost one chapter a week. The group will then have the option of deciding to continue with another study for another 10-12 more weeks.

If you are meeting with your small group each week, consider the group meeting day as the seventh day of the week (that is, begin Day 1 on the day after your small group meeting day).

At the end of each chapter is a section entitled: "Taking It Further: Small Group and Chapter Summary Questions." I suggest that small groups begin their discussions with these summary questions. The group can use any or all of these questions, and any questions in the chapter which the participants want to discuss. Of course, the group members will also have some of their own questions and issues. I advise that groups not feel the need to begin with Day 1 and move methodically through the seven days of the chapter, attempting to address each question. Be flexible with the curriculum and how it is approached and discussed.

Focus on relationships rather than on the completion of the intended agenda. Allow discussion to go where it needs to go, according to the needs of the group.

We have found that smaller groups (with 3-6 participants) provide the best environment for spiritual growth. Small groups are how Christians experience *koinonia* (intimate, supportive fellowship), and walk together and support each other in their faith journeys. The Christian Church needs both expressions of church as described in the Acts 2 community: gathering for worship in the temple (large group) as well as gathering in homes for the breaking of the bread (Acts 2:46). For congregations that want to grow in faith, spirit, and mission, small groups will need to become an essential part of the congregational structure, not just an additional activity for those who like to participate in small groups.

Small groups will typically have these components: time for prayer, time to share how life is going (and support of each other), time for Bible study, and time for discussion of the weekly chapter.

Small groups have been the environment in which many people of Peace Lutheran have learned to pray aloud with each other. We learn to pray with others by practicing praying with and for others. Consider a variety of prayer methods to encourage growth in prayer (read prayers, written prayers, circle prayers, sentence prayers, spontaneous prayer, prayer journals, among many other methods.[86]

A small group covenant helps a group agree to expectations and accountability. (See below for suggestions.)

Everyone in the group should be encouraged to share, but should not be pressured to do so. There is no need for each person to provide his or her answers to each question that is discussed. The group should learn not to rush to fill in the silences.

People will have different perspectives, experiences, and interpretations of the Bible.

Group members should agree not to attempt to give advice or fix one another's problems, unless asked for help. This is not a therapy group.

The use of "I statements" (rather than "you," "we," or "they") helps participants to avoid speaking for or about others.

Groups need to decide when and if new members are to be welcomed into the group.

Confidentiality is essential for a group to have a foundation of honesty and to build trust.

The group should agree to a shared leadership unless one person is appointed as the convener. In this case, the convener can lead and model leadership of the weekly meeting for a few weeks until the group is ready to share and rotate the leadership.

A Small Group Covenant

A small group covenant can be a helpful way of clarifying the group's expectations as well as building the group's accountability. A covenant should include agreement to these kinds of commitments:

completion of the weekly assignment;
participation in the weekly group gathering;
maintaining an environment of honesty, trust, and confidentiality;
daily time with God;
prayer for each other during the week.

A sample small group covenant is found below. The small group should agree to the meeting schedule and any logistics.

A Sample Small Group Covenant[87]

Purpose of the group: In order to grow in Christ, walk together, and support each other, we give ourselves to this small group opportunity, praying that the Holy Spirit will use it and grow us for God's purpose.

We agree to these commitments:

- to read and complete the weekly assignment;
- to regularly participate in the weekly group gathering;
- to maintain an environment of honesty, trust, and confidentiality;
- to spend daily time with God;
- to pray for each other during the week.

Our small group will meet weekly according to this schedule:

Our small group will exist together for this intended length of time:

______ten to twelve weeks.

______ten weeks, and then perhaps another ten weeks…

______one year

Signed: ____

Names and phone numbers/email addresses of group members

Discipleship Groups of 3 and 4

In 2004, Peace Lutheran Church, Charlottesville, Virginia, began its first discipleship group of four men. Although related to the developing mission of the congregation, it did not really arise from an intentional implementation of a vision or mission objective. In a search for small group resources, I came across Greg Ogden's book, *Transforming Discipleship*, and his long term approach to spiritual growth in the congregation was an intriguing concept. I came to agree with Ogden's conclusion that discipleship groups of 3-4 persons are the optimal size for the discipling process.[88]

Ogden argues that small groups of three or four people provide the best environment for discipling people in the faith; small groups of three or four people best provide the three essential ingredients for transformation: the Word of God (the appropriation of scriptural truth), transparent, trusting relationships ("the extent to which we are willing to reveal to others those areas of our life that need God's transforming touch is the extent to which we are inviting the Holy Spirit to make us new"), and mutual accountability (encouraging and holding each other accountable to the discipleship covenant to which they have agreed).[89]

To clarify, a small group of 3-4 persons will have an advantage over a larger group of 6-10 people, in that self-disclosure and openness become "increasingly difficult in direct proportion to the size of the group," and "greater numbers decrease access to a person's life."[90] In other words, the larger the group, the more likely one can hide, in terms of group discussion, sharing one's life, and fulfilling the covenant. When a group has only three or four persons, full participation by all is both necessary and obvious. The fact that most discipleship groups meet together for at least a year helps to develop the transparent trust and accountability, and over the course of a year group members will give and receive the care of Christ though life's highs and lows. The group members will be able to support and care for one another through the natural rhythm of periods of grief and difficulty as well as joys and celebrations ("If one member suffers, all suffer together with it; if one member is honored, all rejoice together with it" 1 Corinthians 12:26).

Discipleship groups at Peace Lutheran Church have been groups of 3-4 persons (either men's or women's groups) which typically meet together weekly, for at least 90 minutes, for prayer, discussion about the biblical readings and workbook questions, and fellowship and care for each other. The convener calls the group together and models the leadership for a few sessions, and then the group rotates with a shared leadership. All share an equal responsibility, and no one person is the "teacher."

Discipleship groups have been a most significant step in developing a congregational culture of discipleship. Discipleship groups have become stepping stones into other faith-forming experiences (small groups, Bible studies, retreats, and mission trips) which invite people to step out of their comfort zones and to place themselves into new contexts which invite them to be open to God and to other people. What has been experienced by the people of Peace is that God uses this stepping into a new experience as a way to bring about spiritual growth.

Endnotes

[1]John D. Herman, Growing Disciples: The Impact of Discipleship Groups on the Spiritual Vitality of a Congregation, 2. Thesis (D. Min.) – The Lutheran Theological Seminary at Philadelphia, 2011.

[2]Brian McLaren, A Search for What is Real, (Grand Rapids, MI: Zondervan, 2007), 54-56.

[3]Craig Barnes, Yearning: Living between How It Is & How It Ought to Be. (Downers Grove, IL: InterVarsity Press, 1992), 50.

[4]Ibid, 56.

[5]C. S. Lewis, Mere Christianity. (New York: Macmillan Pub. Co, 1984), 46.

[6]Brian McLaren, A Search for What Makes Sense, (Grand Rapids, MI: Zondervan, 2007), 115.

[7]Why was there such an altar? According to Athenian legend, a deadly plague was overcome centuries earlier when the Athenians set loose a flock of sheep within the city. "Wherever the sheep were found, they were slain and sacrificed as an offering to a god. If a sheep was slain near an altar of a recognized god, the people dedicated that sacrifice to that god. But if a sheep was slain where there was no altar nearby, an altar was quickly erected and the animal was sacrificed to an unknown god. Ray Stedman, God's Unfinished Book: Adventuring Through the Book of Acts. (Grand Rapids: MI: Discovery House Publishers, 2008), 229.

[8]Ibid.

[9]Ibid., 230.

[10]Barnes, Yearning, 20.

[11]Evangelical Lutheran Church in America and Evangelical Lutheran Church in Canada, Evangelical Lutheran Worship. (Minneapolis, MN: Augsburg Fortress, 2009), 44.

[12]Ibid., 54-55.

[13]Walter Brueggemann. 2010. "Have you heard the good news?" Sojourners Magazine 39, no. 11:48-49.

[14]ELW, 76.

[15]Kent Annan, Following Jesus through the Eye of a Needle: Living Fully, Loving Dangerously. (Downers Grove, IL: IVP Books, 2009), 52-53.

[16]Richard Foster, Life With God: Reading the Bible for Spiritual Transformation. (New York: HarperCollins, 2010), 44-45.

[17]Ibid.

[18]Steven James, Never the Same: Stories of Those Who Encountered Jesus. (Grand Rapids, MI: Zondervan, 2005), 9.

[19]Adapted from John P. Bowen, Evangelism for "Normal" People: Good News for Those Looking for a Fresh Approach. (Minneapolis: Augsburg Fortress, 2002), 135.

[20]Norma Cook Everist and Craig L. Nessan. Transforming Leadership: New Vision for a Church in Mission. (Minneapolis: Fortress Press, 2008), p. 203.

[21]Richard H. Bliese and Graig Van Gelder, The Evangelizing Church: A Lutheran Contribution. (Minneapolis, MN: Augsburg Fortress Press, 2005), 15.

[22]Ibid., 11.

[23]Bowen, 129.

[24]This list is adapted from Marcus Borg, The Heart of Christianity: Rediscovering a Life of Faith. (San Francisco: HarperSanFrancisco, 2003), 168.

[25]Glenn McDonald, The Disciple Making Church: From Dry Bones to Spiritual Vitality. (Grand Haven, MI: FaithWalk Pub, 2004), 142.

[26]Mars Hill. Narrative Theology. http://marshill.org/believe/about/narrative-theology/ (accessed 12/12/11)

[27]James, Never the Same, 10.

[28]McDonald, 135.

[29]Ibid.

[30]Barbara Brown Taylor, Gospel Medicine, (Cambridge, MA: Cowley Publications, 1995), 15.

[31]Dietrich Bonhoeffer, The Cost of Discipleship, (New York: Touchstone, 1995), 89.

[32]Taylor, 17.

[33]This is also translated as "born again," or "born anew." I prefer the translation "born from above," because it hints at where the gift of spiritual rebirth comes from.

[34]Fred B. Craddock, John. (Atlanta: John Knox Press, 1982), 30.

[35]Marjorie J. Thompson, Melissa Tidwell, and John Indermark, Companions in Christ: The Way of Grace, (Nashville, TN: Upper Room Books, 2004), 39.

[36]ELW, 27.

[37]Barbara Brown Taylor. 1996. "Stay for tea, Nicodemus." Christian Century 113, no. 6: 195.

[38]Ibid.

[39]Ibid.

[40]Kenneth E. Bailey, Jesus Through Middle Eastern Eyes: Cultural Studies in the Gospels. (Downers Grove, IL: IVP Academic, 2008), 200-216.

[41]Randy Frazee, The Connecting Church: Beyond Small Groups to Authentic Community. (Grand Rapids, MI: Zondervan Pub. House, 2001), 13.

[42]Andy Stanley and Bill Willets, Creating Community, (Portland OR: Multnomah, 2004), 20.

[43]Companions in Christ, 46.

[44]John Ortberg, Laurie Pederson, and Judson Poling, Groups: The Life-Giving Power of Community. (Grand Rapids, MI: Zondervan, 2000), 52-53.

[45]Companions in Christ, 51.

[46]Lynne Hybels and Bill Hybels, Rediscovering Church: The Story and Vision of Willow Creek Community Church. (Grand Rapids, MI: Zondervan Pub. House, 1995), 159.

[47]Virginia Rickeman, The Well is Deep: Prayers to Draw Up Living Water. (Cleveland, Ohio: United Church Press, 1999), 99.

[48]Dietrich Bonhoeffer, Life Together. (New York: Harper, 1954), 115.

[49]Bailey, Jesus Through Middle Eastern Eyes, 215.

[50]Daily Discipleship. Third Sunday in Lent (A) – John 4:5-42. http://www.elca.org/Growing-In-Faith/Discipleship/Christian-Education/Daily-Discipleship/Full-Lectionary/Year-A-Qtr-2.aspx (accessed 12/12/11)

[51]ELW, 27.

[52]Craddock, John, sets this story in six scenes.

[53]Craddock, John, 71.

[54]Richard Lischer. 1999. "Acknowledgment." Christian Century 116, no.7: 245.

[55]Margaret Nutting Ralph, Discovering the Gospels: Four Accounts of the Good News. (New York: Paulist Press, 1990), 237.

[56]Lischer.

[57]David H. Stern, Jewish New Testament Commentary: A Companion Volume to the Jewish New Testament. (Clarksville, MD: Jewish New Testament Publications, 1992), 181.

[58]Companions in Christ, 68.

[59]ELW, 47.

[60]Bailey, Jesus Through Middle Eastern Eyes, 234.

[61]Ray C. Stedman, "Judging the Judges." ww.raystedman.org/new-testament/john/judging-the-judges (accessed 12/12/11)

[62]Liz Curtis Higgs, Really Bad Girls of the Bible: More Lessons from Less-Than-Perfect Women. (Colorado Springs, CO: Waterbrook Press, 2000), 84.

[63]Ibid., 89.

[64]N. T. Wright, Luke for Everyone. (London: SPCK, 2004), 91.

[65]Fred B. Craddock, Luke. (Louisville,KY: John Knox Press, 1990), 105.

[66]Martin Luther, Large Catechism: Lord's Prayer, 90-91, in Robert Kolb, Timothy J. Wengert, and Charles P. Arand. The Book of Concord: The Confessions of the Evangelical Lutheran Church. Minneapolis: Fortress Press, 2000.

[67]Don N. Howell, Servants of the Servant: A Biblical Theology of Leadership. (Eugene, OR: Wipf & Stock Publishers, 2003), 206.

[68]ELW, 55.

[69]Ibid., 210.

[70]Ibid., 211.

[71]Companions in Christ, 103.

[72]Virginia Rickeman, The Well is Deep, 115.

[73]Shelly Rubel, God Responds to All Who Seek Him in David Fleer and Dave Bland, Preaching the Sermon on the Mount: The World It Imagines. (Saint Louis, MO: Chalice Press, 2007), 161.

[74]Adapted from the prayer, Commitment in ELW, 86.

[75]Kenneth E. Bailey, Through Peasant Eyes: More Lucan Parables, Their Culture and Style. (Grand Rapids, MI: W.B. Eerdmans Pub. Co, 1980), 26-27.

[76]Ibid., 28.

[77]Rob Bell, Nooma. 013 Rich. (Grand Rapids, MI: Zondervan, 2006).

[78]Brian P. Stoffregen, Mark 10.17-31. Proper 23-Year B. http://www.crossmarks.com/brian/mark10x17.htm

[79]N.T. Wright, Mark for Everyone. (London: SPCK, 2004), 135.

[80]Jesus leaves out the command which prohibited coveting. "Coveting is the disease of always wanting more, and it's rooted in a profound dissatisfaction with the life God has given you. Coveting is what happens when you aren't at peace." Rob Bell, Love Wins: A Book About Heaven, Hell, and the Fate of Every Person Who Ever Lived. (New York, NY: HarperOne, 2011), 41.

[81]James, Never the Same, 68.

[82]Bell, 41.

[83]Rickeman, 17.

[84]My daughter, Kristin Langholz, provides this concluding thought.

[85]Rickeman, 17.

[86]For guidance in developing prayer, see "Prayer in small groups" in Augsburg Fortress (Publisher), Starting Small Groups – and Keeping Them Going. (Minneapolis, Augsburg Fortress, 1995), 120.

[87]Sample small group covenants can be found in Greg Ogden, Discipleship Essentials: A Guide to Building Your Life in Christ. (Downers Grove, IL: IVP Connect, 2007), 14, and in Starting Small Groups – and Keeping Them Going, 121.

[88]Greg Ogden, Transforming Discipleship: Making Disciples a Few at a Time. (Downers Grove, IL: InterVarsity, 2003), 171-72.

[89]Greg Ogden, Making Disciples Jesus' Way: A Few At A Time, 2007. http://www.gregogden.com/PDFs/TransformingDiscipleshipSummary.pdf (accessed 9/20/10).

[90]Greg Ogden, Discipleship Essentials, 11.

Made in the USA
Columbia, SC
20 January 2018